THE PRIVATE PASSION OF

JACKIE KENNEDY ONASSIS

ALSO BY VICKY MOON

The Official Middleburg Life Cookbook

The Middleburg Mystique

Best Dressed Southern Salads

A Sunday Horse

THE PRIVATE PASSION OF

JACKIE KENNEDY ONASSIS

Portrait of a Rider

VICKY MOON

REGANBOOKS

Grateful acknowledgment is made for permission to reprint the following copyrighted material:

"Horse Talk" on pages 52 to 55: Hunting terms from "Riding to Hounds in America" by William P. Wadsworth,

MFH. Reprinted by permission from *The Chronicle of the Horse*, Middleburg, Virginia 20118.

Call (800) 877-5467 to subscribe. Copyright © by 1987 *The Chronicle of the Horse*.

Letter from Grampy Jack on page 47: From *Jacqueline Bouvier Kennedy* by Mary Van Rensselaer Thayer, page 29.

Reprinted by permission from Random House, Inc. Published by Doubleday and Company, Garden City, New York.

Copyright © 1961 by Mary Van Rensselaer Thayer.

FIRST EDITION

Printed on acid-free paper

Library of Congress Cataloging-in-Publication Data

Moon, Vicky.
   The private passion of Jackie Kennedy Onassis : portrait of a rider / Vicky Moon—1st ed.
      p. cm.
   ISBN 0-06-052411-1
      1. Onassis, Jacqueline Kennedy, 1929– 2. Horsemen and horsewomen—United States—Biography. 3. Celebrities—
United States—Biography. 4. Presidents' spouses—United States—Biography. I. Title.

SF284.52.O52M66 2004
798.2'092—dc22
[B]   2004046777

05 06 07 08 09 ❖/TP 10 9 8 7 6 5 4 3 2 1

BOOK DESIGN AND LAYOUT JUDITH STAGNITTO ABBATE / ABBATE DESIGN

FOR MY MOTHER, NAOMA REES MOON,

FOR ALL THINGS HORSEY, AND SO MUCH MORE.

Contents

Preface   xv

Preface

I WAS SEVEN YEARS OLD WHEN I DISCOVERED
MY MOTHER'S TALL, WORN-OUT BLACK
RIDING BOOTS TUCKED HIGH IN A CORNER

of the closet. Of course, I pulled them down, shined them, and tromped around in them for hours. Horseback riding lessons, that's what I wanted. I eventually wore down my parents and began to live for Saturday group lessons at Mrs. Elliott's in Davie, Florida.

To this day, I can tell you the names of all the horses and ponies I fell in love with: Pepper, Flame, and Trio. After about two years of begging, I became the proud owner of Pepito, a feisty chestnut pony. Next was Midnight. Then there was Tom-tom and The Villager. My father, who was footing the bills for my equine passion, kept repeating to anyone who would listen, "This is only a passing fancy. Once she discovers boys, that will be it." By the time I owned a big strapping chestnut named Tom Collins, I'd been married once and divorced.

When it comes to horses, there is no such thing as a passing fancy. They're a constant in life.

OPPOSITE JULY 4, 1938: OFFICIALS MURRAY MCDONNELL, RICHARD NEWTON, AND RANDALL POINDEXTER PREPARE TO ANNOUNCE THE RESULTS AS JACKIE AND DANSEUSE WAIT. MCDONNELL REMAINED A LIFELONG FRIEND OF JACKIE.

COMPANIONSHIP

1929-1952

ALMOST EVERY LITTLE GIRL DREAMS ABOUT OWNING A PONY, BUT FOR JACQUELINE BOUVIER, IT WAS A GIVEN.

Jackie's mother first propped her on a horse at the tender age of one. In the privileged circle into which she was born, riding was a necessary social grace, as was playing a decent game of tennis, knowing which fork to use, and writing a proper thank-you note.

But what many people still don't realize is how vital a role horses played throughout Jackie's often star-crossed life. As a little girl longing to see her elusive father, she found companionship and comfort with her pony Buddy. As a woman aching for the presence of her husband and burdened with the crushing pressures of her role as First Lady, riding a horse through the wide-open countryside brought sanctuary. Later in life, the lonely widow and reluctant celebrity found anonymity and solace in riding. Her time spent alone with her horses was her private passion. As one family member recalled, "I did not realize it at the time, but I now believe her obsession with horses stemmed from her desperately unhappy home life."

OPPOSITE JULY 26, 1933: JACKIE AND HER MOTHER IN THE FAMILY CLASS AT THE EAST HAMPTON HORSE SHOW. AS PART OF THEIR EFFORTS TO "MATCH," THE HORSES HAVE IDENTICAL BROWBANDS ON THE BRIDLE.

PREVIOUS SPREAD JACKIE WITH ONE OF HER FIRST PONIES, BUDDY, IN AUGUST 1934 AT THE SOUTHAMPTON HORSE SHOW.

Jackie's mother, Janet Norton Lee, married stockbroker and ne'er-do-well John Vernou Bouvier III at St. Philomena's Church in East Hampton on July 7, 1928. It was a grand affair with flowing champagne, luscious cake, and 500 guests.

Jacqueline Lee Bouvier was born a year later on July 28, 1929, at the Southampton Hospital, not far from where her parents were married. The family settled into an apartment on Park Avenue in Manhattan, New York, and spent summers with their horses on Long Island. Their ties to the Hamptons on the eastern end of Long Island were strong. The summer seasons of Jackie's youth revolved around socializing at the Maidstone Club and the Devon Yacht Club, romping on the dunes, fishing near Montauk Point, and attending polo matches and endless soirees.

The charming and chic resort area of Long Island was peppered with windmills, small ponds, and cedar shake cottages. William Steinkraus, a member of the United States Equestrian Team (USET) from 1951–1972 and the first

RIGHT JACKIE AND HER MOTHER JANET BOUVIER, SHOWN HERE IN SEPTEMBER 1933, OFTEN RODE IN THE PARENT-CHILD CLASS.

American to win an individual gold medal in show-jumping in 1968, recalled traveling to the Hamptons for the horse shows. He said it was like "going to the country with no sense of encroaching suburbia."

Jackie's paternal grandparents, Maude and John Vernou Bouvier Jr., summered on Further Lane in East Hampton at the twelve-acre Lasata, an Indian word for "place of peace." In addition to a four-car garage, there was the requisite stable, riding ring, tack room, and paddocks. The nameplates of the Bouvier horses adorned each stall: Ghandi, Stepaside, Pas d'Or, Arnoldean, and Danseuse. After formal Sunday luncheons of Long Island duckling and applesauce, Jackie would run to the stables. These were happy times for the young girl, times spent with wonderful horses and her beloved Grampy Jack.

One of the final events of the season was the East Hampton Horse Show, held each August at the East Hampton Riding Club. The club, an offshoot of the majestic, circa 1891 Maidstone Club, was founded in 1924, when the "old Baker farm" on Pantigo Lane was bought from John Dickinson. The clubhouse was renovated and furnished with area antiques. A history of the club recounts, "Stabling and grooms' quarters are unusually elaborate and substantial for a summer club." There was a main riding ring and an outside course. The history continues, "The clubhouse is open to members for cozy afternoon teas beside an open fire."

Janet Bouvier served as president of the horse show and was a joint master of the Suffolk Hounds. She exhibited an elegant manner when she showed a sixteen-hand black gelding named Show Me in the ladies side saddle class. And she made every effort to pass along her love of horses. For Jacqueline's second birthday party, the little guests were treated to pony rides.

By the age of three, Jackie was seriously learning to ride on a pony named Rusty. This is the phase of lessons horse-people refer to as "up/down."

At a young age, one of the most difficult maneuvers is learning to post while the pony or horse is trotting. The rider must rise up out of the saddle in coordination with each step. The riding teacher must constantly repeat the mantra of "up/down" as the rider struggles to acquire the horse's rhythm. Jackie had to master holding two reins in her little hands. At the same time, she received the reminders: "heels down, eyes up, back straight."

Jackie also learned to ride on a miniature horse called Jerry. Cousin John Davis once wrote, "she smelled of horses...sweat and horsehair laced with manure." And not long after that came Buddy, a beloved dark brown pony with a little bit of white on his left hind foot.

While Jackie perfected her horsemanship, Mrs. Bouvier rode in the East Hampton show each summer. She won the Newell J. Ward Challenge Cup riding Arnoldean in 1931, a championship competition for members of the club. The horses were judged "in hand," meaning they were analyzed for their physical structure and shape. Thirty years later, Jackie would find herself as a guest of Mrs. Newell J. Ward for an afternoon at the steeplechase races in Virginia. Her horse connections were lifelong and very strong.

The East Hampton Horse Show program sold for fifty cents. The Mellons, Guggenheims, and Appletons all entered horses. There were advertisements from Stadler & Stadler on Fifth Avenue in New York City, tailors of scarlet field coats; and the always essential Jeanne Coiffeuse beauty shop announced its seasonal move to Newton Lane in East Hampton from the Drake Hotel on Park Avenue. Rodney Jackson's Hampton Air Service of the 1930s offered a forty-minute flight to New York for eight dollars.

In the 1932 East Hampton event, Janet Bouvier was in the winner's circle for the ladies hunter class and the Harry Hamlin Challenge Cup. The exquisite two-handled silver cup was embellished with berries and laurel leaves. It was fifteen inches high and made by Gorham

and Company in Providence, Rhode Island. Janet Bouvier won it three times and eventually it became hers to keep.

"Janet Bouvier not only rode her horses expertly, but she also schooled them so perfectly and loved them so much that they truly became family pets," Mary Van Rensselaer Thayer noted in her 1961 book *Jacqueline Bouvier Kennedy*.

In 1933, Janet won a hunter class as well as the hunt teams event, where three riders perform together. Her accomplishments were widely touted, even with inevitable falls from time to time. And her triumphs were not confined to the East Hampton Horse Show. Riding a Virginia-bred chestnut mare named Danseuse, she won a blue ribbon and a large, circular sterling silver bowl for the Thoroughbred hunter class at the Brookville Horse Show. Sixty years later, at the Jacqueline Kennedy Onassis estate sale in New York, this trophy fetched $14,950 after a pre-sale estimate of $250–$500.

Janet Bouvier brought home four trophies from the 1934 horse show. She rode Danseuse in the Corinthian class for members of a recognized hunt. Riders, wearing formal livery, were required to jump four-foot-high fences, which resembled those found in the hunting field—stone wall, gate, post, and rail. This trophy, estimated at $1,200–$1,500, brought $18,400 at the estate sale.

The judge on this occasion was Alfred B. Maclay, who raised and showed horses from his Killearn Farm in Millbrook, New York. He was the founder of the American Society for the Prevention of Cruelty to Animals (ASPCA) Equitation Championships at the National Horse Show at Madison Square Garden, frequently referred to as the Maclay class.

Jackie's long hours of practice and determination paid off on August 18, 1934. Anyone who wanted to watch the show that year paid a general admission of $1.10. They would have seen Jackie and Janet Bouvier take third place in the family class, trotting around the ring, posting in unison on two chestnut horses. The local paper reported, "One of the most attractive riders at Saturday's show, who would have received a blue ribbon if the spectators had had anything to say about the judging, was the five-year-old daughter of Mrs. John Vernou Bouvier III."

At age five, Jackie also took part in the lead line class. This is an event for which all horse-loving parents live. Young riders are led around the ring by mother, father, or family friend. The judges look for proper posture and composure and, truth be known, they often are influenced by who is holding the end of the lead rope.

For this occasion, Jackie's father had the honors. "Black Jack" Bouvier was known as a fastidious fashion plate. His deep, deliberate tan added to his allure, even if he did have a propensity for frequent swigs from his flask. His lusty look helped pave the path toward a bevy of other women. At horse shows, he often wore a pale summer suit set off with a smart tie, a silk pocket square, and the spectator wing tip shoes that were so stylish at the time.

Like most little girls, Jackie probably couldn't sleep the night before the big event, setting out her riding habit and making sure her boots were shined. She wore a boutonniere, soft felt hat, and pint-size gloves and carried a rather long riding crop in her right hand. Her mother, whose refined riding clothes were noted in the local fashion columns such as the "The Social Spectator," always instilled in Jackie the importance of proper attire in and out of the ring. Unfortunately, despite her well-appointed wardrobe, the disappointing results of the lead line were obvious by the pout on little Jackie's face.

"I remember how determined an equestrienne Jacqueline became as she began thirsting after blue ribbons in the many East End horse shows she

OPPOSITE IN 1935 JACKIE RODE IN THE FAMILY CLASS WITH HER COUSIN MICHAEL BOUVIER AT THE EAST HAMPTON HORSE SHOW.

entered," her cousin John H. Davis later wrote. "None of the other Bouvier grandchildren, myself included, had that determination to succeed. We dabbled at golf and tennis and swimming. She really worked at her riding." Her younger sister, Caroline Lee Bouvier, never became quite as mesmerized by riding as Jackie.

The summers were splendid. The *East Hampton Social Guide* announced the arrival of prominent residents and listed summer cottages with the three-digit telephone numbers, along with railroad and ferry timetables. In 1935 Jackie's parents were listed at Rowdy Hall on Egypt Lane. The two-story clapboard had been a boarding house at the corner of Main Street and David's Lane during the 1890s, popular with rowdy night-owl artists who earned it its name.

While sitting on the top rail at the horse show that August, six-year-old Jackie was glued to the competition. She was surrounded by adults: Franklin D'Olier, Winifred Lee, Marian Raymond, and her grandmother, Margaret Lee.

RIGHT JACKIE WATCHES EVERY HORSE AND RIDER AS THEY COME INTO THE RING AT THE SOUTHAMPTON RIDING CLUB HORSE SHOW, AUGUST 11, 1935. FROM LEFT TO RIGHT: FRANKLIN D'OLIER, WINIFRED LEE, JACKIE, MARIAN RAYMOND, AND HER GRANDMOTHER MRS. JAMES T. LEE.

On a hot dusty day, they were all dressed to the teeth and there to be seen, not to see.

"The Hamptons had a certain cachet, even then," recalled veteran gold medalist Steinkraus, "and many spectators were dressed more fashionably than one ordinarily expected of summer horse show attendees."

Little Jacqueline, in jodhpurs and paddock shoes, soaked up every minute. She could tell you the name of every horse and their record. "It was very striking how smart and fashionable the horse sports were on Long Island in those days," Steinkraus explained. "Hunt racing, foxhunting, and polo were very much included. Everybody was beautifully turned out, especially the women, who often hunted sidesaddle and looked smashing on the pages of numerous equine magazines of the day, including *The Sportsman, Country Life, Turf and Paddock,* and of course, *Horse & Horseman.*"

The buildup for the annual horse show in the *East Hampton Star* began every season in late May. One small paragraph in 1936 noted, "The Riding Club of East Hampton will open for the season on Memorial Day. Mrs. Simmons will be there if members wish to take tea." Parking spaces around the main ring sold for eleven dollars.

The Bouvier family returned for a summer in East Hampton in 1936 as the local papers continued to trumpet the horse show, with its $2,500 in cash awards and trophies. "Saturday morning and afternoon promises to be one of the outstanding shows of the Seashore Circuit, and the finest horse show ever held here," William C. Morgan, president of the club, told the paper. (To compare, the Hampton Classic Horse Show, a contemporary sporting and social fixture held every August for the last twenty-five years, currently awards $500,000 in prize money.)

Frances "Fanny" Gardiner, now in her mid-eighties, a member of an old and acclaimed Long Island family, recalled Black Jack Bouvier's grand entrance at the event. "He had a big Duessenberg and he romped into the show grounds with the top down." Tailgating had a genteel flavor, with large whicker hampers and leather-covered flasks. A break from 12:35 to 2 P.M. was scheduled in the official program timetable, right after the Suffolk Hounds Hunter Class and before the Saddle Horses. It was noted in the program, "lunch will be served at the club house on the grounds at one dollar per person." A gala horse show ball at the Maidstone Club concluded the day.

During the 1930s, a coach or trainer was unheard of, and Janet Bouvier took on the role of instructor. The tension between mother and daughter often reflected itself in stern admonitions of proper equestrian style when Janet gave instructions to her pupil. When Jackie fell off Buddy at the Southampton Horse Show, she picked herself up and went about remounting. In the excitement of the moment, she attempted to shimmy back on from the "off" side, the right side of the horse. The left is traditionally proper, dating to the days when soldiers wore their swords on the left side, making it easier to remount. As the ringmaster helped her get back on, spectators applauded.

Mrs. Bouvier didn't react with the expected maternal compassion. Instead, she scolded her daughter for not remounting from the correct side. And she reminded Jackie that her duty was to make sure the pony was not hurt.

The 1936 show season ended on a high note for Janet Bouvier. A front-page headline declared, "Mrs. Bouvier Wins 8 Ribbons At Horse Show." Her chestnut mare, Stepaside, was the most successful local horse again, winning the Harry L. Hamlin Memorial Challenge Cup. It seems East Hampton noses were out of joint when results were tallied and eighty-three of the one hundred awards went to "out-of-towners." Mrs. Julius Bliss of Bronxville, New York, was the biggest winner of the day, capturing two

championships with a gelding called Tupelo.

In the family class, Janet and Jackie Bouvier took fourth place. But the family tension behind the scenes was escalating, and by the beginning of October, Janet and Jack became legally separated. It was a time of tremendous turmoil for Jackie, and according to a family member, she became uncustomarily withdrawn.

During this tumultuous period, riding horses became "a stabilizer," recalled Fanny Gardiner, who observed the stress. "The lives they lived, oh, go here, go there. She could always come back to her horses."

Jackie continued her horse pursuits back in New York while attending the tony Miss Chapin's School. When she became unruly, the headmistress, Miss Ethel Stringfellow, used a horse-oriented analogy to get seven-year-old Jackie's undivided attention. She compared her to an unbroken Thoroughbred. "Even a Thoroughbred, if not disciplined, is destined for failure," she told her. The strategy evidently worked, as Jackie settled into her studies and looked forward to another summer on the Island.

Jackie was eight years old when her parents attempted to reconcile in 1937. Her horses once again provided comfort, as her so-called friends teased and occasionally taunted her over her parents' precarious marriage. The atmosphere at home was "strained and irritable," according to one employee. But Jackie did win a blue ribbon at the annual horse show that summer, riding her Pinto Dance Step in the seat-and-hands class for riders under nine years old. As committee member George Roberts presented the small silver cup, she accepted it as if she had done it many times before.

"I remember her from those shows in Long Island," Steinkraus said. "She was a nice rider and among the East Hampton crowd, she had nice horses and was nicely turned out. She didn't do the whole circuit, which was quite competitive."

PREVIOUS SPREAD JANET BOUVIER GLANCES TO THE SIDE TO ENCOURAGE HER DAUGHTER TO KEEP UP IN THE PARENT-CHILD CLASS OF THE SMITHTOWN HORSE SHOW, SEPTEMBER 1935, IN ST. JAMES, LONG ISLAND.

RIGHT JACKIE AT THE SMITHTOWN HORSE SHOW, AUGUST 28, 1937.

During autumn Janet Bouvier started to make the rounds of the big city cocktail social circuit alone. By the following summer in 1938, Jackie was fully engaged in the tug-of-war between her parents. Her mother at first rented a separate cottage in Bellport, far away from fashionable East Hampton. Before Jackie could adjust to this tense dynamic, her mother moved back in with her father in August. Bewildered by her parents' vacillation, Jackie turned her attention to jumping her lovable chestnut mare Danseuse on the Long Island Circuit, including the Smithtown Horse Show. That August, she had another victory at the East Hampton show.

The spousal acrimony was at fever pitch. Janet and Jack were "at sword points," according to Elizabeth "Lib" Hyland Maloney, one of the top riders of the era. At this point Jack Bouvier knew how to get Janet where it hurt. He could take away her horses.

Lib Maloney was asked to show them. "He kept the horses at his family's stables," she recalled. "He wanted to sell

PREVIOUS SPREAD AUGUST 1937: JACKIE TOOK FIRST PLACE IN A CLASS FOR CHILDREN UNDER NINE YEARS OF AGE ON DANCE STEP. DR. GEORGE ROBERTS PRESENTS THE TROPHY AT THE EAST HAMPTON HORSE SHOW.

RIGHT JACKIE ON HER BELOVED CHESTNUT MARE DANSEUSE, JULY 4, 1938, IN SOUTHAMPTON.

them. It was an ugly situation and the two of them were not speaking." The grooms approached her to ride. "I just got on them and went. The one mare, Danseuse, had a bad knee. She was nervous about it and you couldn't trust her. She didn't want to hit her knee, and if she came into the jump wrong, she'd stop."

Bad knee or not, Danseuse, now known as "Donny," became Jackie's full time mount. Her sister Lee later recalled how Jackie, her father, and the horse were inseparable. Jackie made up a scrapbook of letters when their father died, and Lee estimated at least half of them made some sort of reference to the beloved horse and plans for the horse shows.

For the first time, Jackie continued on the Long Island circuit past Labor Day, traveling out from the city on the weekends. Perhaps it was a special treat from her adoring father, who now controlled the horses. She rode at the Piping Rock Horse Show in Locust Valley. She appeared happy and content while sitting on a tack trunk at the Boulder Brook Horse Show.

Lib Maloney also rode for Richard K. Mellon (a cousin of Paul Mellon) and completed the season on the Bouvier horse Stepaside, advancing all the way to the National Horse Show at Madison Square Garden. She won the $1,000 Hunter Stake and was Reserve Champion Hunter. In one photo, Janet Bouvier, wrapped in mink, gazes in the distance and Maloney looks at the horse. "Janet Bouvier never got on that horse again," Maloney added. The mare was sold to Peggy Klipstein, then a student at Greenwich Academy.

When they returned to the city in 1938, Janet moved with her daughters to One Gracie Square, close to Miss Chapin's School. She retaliated against her husband by hiring detectives to follow him. Not long after that, his infidelities became big news in the papers. Jackie was devastated. But her father continued to indulge her horse habit. Not quite

OPPOSITE MALONEY RODE STEPASIDE TO FIRST PLACE IN THE LADIES WORKING HUNTER CLASS AT THE FAIRFIELD COUNTY HUNT CLUB HORSE SHOW IN JUNE 1939.

Lib & Mrs. J. V. Bouvier
"STEPASIDE" Winner
of Hunter Stake &
Reserve Champion
Hunter
National Horse Show
Madison Sq. Garden
November 1938

ten years old, Jackie began showing much earlier in the season in 1939, starting out at the Vassar Horse Show in May on Danseuse.

Jackie appeared resigned to her parents' doomed marriage. Her life was filled with diversionary horse-related activities. Just after her tenth birthday, Jackie went to watch the horse show in Tuxedo Park with her mother. Seated in a grandstand box, the horse-loving young girl leaned over the rail, oblivious to the photographer snapping her photo. Her mother and Mrs. Allen McLane were also captured, seemingly more aware that the moment was being recorded.

One paper reported Jackie as Long Island's youngest horse show fan, spotted at "every important contest for several seasons." Although she was still too inexperienced to equal her mother's horse show conquests, she eventually would go on to exceed Janet's accomplishments. It became a complicated mother-daughter relationship—with a well-documented competition between them for the affection of Jackie's father. Some have even referred to it as "semi-incestuous." Her mother was often indignant toward and jealous of her oldest child, which gave Jackie all the more reason to turn to her horses for solace. The only constants in her life remained the horses and the horse shows, year after year.

The *East Hampton Star* published all the significant summer events: notable weddings, garden tours, and results of key golf, backgammon, and skeet tournaments. In the middle of the front page on July 27, 1939, a headline reads: "New Classes Add Interest to 15th E.H. Horse Show." The article elaborates: "The riding club of East Hampton is making extensive preparations for the fifteenth annual Horse Show on August 12. Mrs. Janet Lee-Bouvier heads the executive committee, aided by Mmes. Shepard Krech, Harry Hamlin,

OPPOSITE CHAMPION HORSEWOMAN ELIZABETH MALONEY. SHOWN HERE WITH JANET BOUVIER, RODE STEPASIDE TO FIRST PLACE AT THE NATIONAL HORSE SHOW AT MADISON SQUARE GARDEN IN NOVEMBER 1938.

Shults Dougherty, Frank P. Shepard, and George Roberts; also Walter B. Duryea, Dr. Krech, George L. McAlpin Jr., William C. Morgan, Richard Newton Jr., M.F.H. [Master of Foxhounds], and Robert Schey."

The highlight at the horse show that year was the fancy dress class, always a favorite with the children. Fanny Gardiner vividly remembered the event more than sixty years later. "Jackie chose an Indian costume because she was riding a black and white Indian pony," she said. She rode bareback with an Indian style blanket. (And for anyone alarmed by what appears to be a swastika-like design on the costume, not to worry; it was an ancient Indian emblem of the sun.) This event always had a particularly special meaning to Jackie, and she'd later help her own daughter Caroline dress up and compete, too.

Gardiner, like most horse-loving girls, still maintains her infatuation with horses with a small stable and several horses on ten acres near Three Mile Harbor in East

RIGHT JACKIE LOOKS TO THE NEXT JUMP AS DANSEUSE LANDS OVER A JUMP AT THE SOUTHAMPTON HORSE SHOW ON JULY 29, 1939.

PREVIOUS SPREAD JACQUELINE BOUVIER WITH MRS. ALLEN MCLANE AND JANET BOUVIER AT THE TUXEDO PARK HORSE SHOW, JUNE 2, 1939.

Hampton. Back then, she dressed as a scarecrow. "I turned my brother's tailcoat inside out and shoved it full of hay," she recalled. She embellished her costume with cowboy boots and overalls. "The judge walked up and asked, 'Is anybody in there?' Back then, it was all for fun. Sometimes we would ride with no saddle and no bridle and jump without hands."

Janet Bouvier was finally granted her divorce from Black Jack in 1940, after spending the required six weeks in Reno. And where had she spent the six weeks? At the Lazy A Bar Ranch, where Janet, Jackie, and Lee galloped on the range riding western on Jim, Banjo, and Wagstaff. Jackie, now eleven years old, had an abbreviated visit to East Hampton and won the equitation class for children from ages eleven to thirteen. She returned to New York City, where she'd visit with her father on Sundays, taking long walks in Central Park and a few trips to Belmont Park for the horse races.

In 1941 the price of hay was advertised for thirty-five dollars a ton in the *Chronicle of the Horse,* a weekly sporting publication and horse lovers' sacred publication for sixty-five years. A ton in today's market would run between $165–$300. "Man O' War Body Brace" claimed to leave "the coat and skin of your horse in a clean sparkling condition" for six dollars a gallon. Clothing was listed under haberdashery, with Harris tweeds and Shetland sweaters the most popular apparel. And another small column also catches the eye: "Miss Peggy Klipstein of Greenwich, Connecticut, would like to sell her hunter Stepaside due to going away to college. Priced right."

One of the most prestigious events for a young rider (under age seventeen) to win is the equitation class known as the ASPCA Horsemanship Championship.

OPPOSITE AUGUST 12, 1939: JACKIE DRESSED AS AN INDIAN WON A RIBBON IN THE COSTUME CLASS WITH DANCE STEP AT THE EAST HAMPTON RIDING CLUB.

PREVIOUS SPREAD OVER SIXTY YEARS LATER, FRANCES "FANNY" GARDINER STILL REMEMBERS WHEN SHE DRESSED IN HER BROTHER'S TAILCOAT AS A SCARECROW AND RODE IN THE EAST HAMPTON HORSE SHOW ALONG WITH JACKIE AS AN INDIAN ON DANCE STEP AND JAY SPALDING AS A COWBOY.

The trophy was donated by Alfred B. Maclay, the esteemed judge at the 1934 East Hampton Horse Show. Many winners have gone on to capture major grand prix jumping events and Olympic medals. In 1941 Jackie Bouvier won a qualifying class at the Southampton Horse Show. Twelve-year-old Jackie could now compete in the national finals at Madison Square Garden. The jumps were three and one-half feet. The horse's performance as such did not count, but the rider's form and finesse were paramount. "The purpose of this event is to emphasize to young riders the importance of kindness and gentleness in handling their mounts," explained the program.

It was an intriguing list of riders for the ASPCA on Saturday morning, November 8, 1941. Miss Jacqueline Bouvier was listed right before Miss Ethel Skakel, who would later become Jackie's sister-in-law as Mrs. Robert Kennedy.

OPPOSITE JACKIE AND DANSEUSE AT THE PIPING ROCK HORSE SHOW, SEPTEMBER 30, 1939, IN LOCUST VALLEY, LONG ISLAND.

Jack Lee Payne, another competitor, became a great horseman in Virginia. And Miss Eve Prime, later Eve Fout, became one of Jackie's lifelong friends in Middleburg. (Playwright Edward Albee and raconteur William F. Buckley Jr. were also show exhibitors, although not in the same event.)

Audrey Hasler Chesney was the first champion in the ASPCA in 1933. She also rode Danseuse for Janet Bouvier at the 1933 Lennox Horse Show in Massachusetts. "I remember the horses were shipped in on a boxcar, and the train would stop to unload them," she said. "It was nothing fancy."

Steinkraus, the eventual winner in 1941, recalled Jackie was not among the final twenty chosen by the judges for the ride-off in the afternoon. (Other books have mistakenly given the impression Jackie won the championship.) Hunter seat equitation back then was still in its infancy and judging form over fences was just emerging. "The equitation division was much less evolved than it is today,"

said Steinkraus. "But it was still very competitive."

Competing at "The Garden," regardless of the outcome, has always been a thrill for any rider. The horses were unloaded off the van onto the sidewalk along West Forty-ninth Street at the "old" Garden, right next to the pretzel vendors. They were stabled in the same building where world famous heavyweight prize fighters Joe Louis and Sugar Ray Robinson dressed for their own title fights at this venerated sports complex.

Men in the box seats were often dressed in white-tie, accompanied by women in glittering long gowns. Society conductor Meyer Davis struck up his band as soon as the five-gaited horses strutted their stuff. (The same orchestra played at Janet's second wedding and later at an inauguration ball when John F. Kennedy became president in 1960.) "The horse show ran a full eight days, Tuesday through Tuesday," Steinkraus remembered. There was a military influence, too, because the 1941 show came one month before Pearl Harbor. In fact, the show was for the benefit of the USO. Jackie loved the National Horse Show, as all horse lovers do. She made it a point to return with her children or friends on several other occasions, but only as a spectator.

When Janet Lee Bouvier married Hugh D. Auchincloss Jr., a socially prominent Washington broker, in June of 1942, there were several perks for Jackie in the form of more riding opportunities. She spent two years at the Holton Arms School in Georgetown, near their forty-six-acre Merrywood Farm just across the Potomac River in McLean, Virginia. For the teenage girl, riding horses almost every day was heaven.

The extended Auchincloss family now spent summers in Newport, Rhode Island at the seventy-five-acre Hammersmith Farm. Jackie once again attended the horse show in East Hampton, participating in the costume class in jockey silks. The thirteen-year-old girl had sprouted a curvaceous figure beneath her riding attire.

After her annual visit to Long Island, Jackie begged her father to send her horse to Rhode Island for the summers. Cousin John Davis later recounted, "Jack [Bouvier] feared that losing control of Jacqueline's beloved mare would mean losing control of his daughter." His drinking problems had intensified as he spent less time with Jackie.

The grand summers of her youth were a thing of the past. In August 1943 the *East Hampton Star* dutifully reported the sale of the East Hampton Horse Show grounds under the headline: "Riding Club's Property Sold to Wm. Scibeck." The price was not recorded, and it was noted the land would be used for farming. The bones of the once bustling horse show can still be found along what is now called Montauk Highway, Route 27.

In the fall of 1944, at the impressionable age of fifteen, Jackie was enrolled at Miss Porter's School. The

fashionable girl's boarding school in Farmington, Connecticut, had been founded by Sarah Porter in 1843, and included a classic curriculum of history, math, English, and proper foreign languages. It oozed upper-crust tradition.

Athletics included the country club sports of tennis, squash, golf, and, of course, horseback riding. Once settled into school, Jackie yearned for her horse. Years later, she confessed to her Georgetown dressmaker Mini Rhea of writing poems to Grampy Jack begging to have her horse stabled at the school. "I paid Grampy with poems," she once said. "Or shall I call a bribe a bribe?"

It worked. He replied in a letter:

What in one aspect might be viewed as a sumptuary extravagance may, on the other hand, from the mental and physical standpoint, be regarded as a justifiable necessity. Within this generalization

naturally falls Danseuse. Psychologically she aids you. Spiritually she provides a wholesome release from sordid worldly cares. Therefore I will engage to meet her keep of $25 a month until April next.

Are you or am I in these dreadful days justified in such an indulgence? I think not, but with the necessity for maintaining Danseuse, both of us are in concurrence.

Jackie spent hours in the stall grooming the mare. She consigned every spare moment to her horse. She reported in letters the horse was between two others in a box stall and very happy. When the weather turned frigid she did what any pampered prep school girl might do. She yanked a blanket off another horse and put it on her own.

Following her successful plea to Grampy Jack, Jackie's horse training

OPPOSITE JACKIE WITH THE HORSES STABLED AT MERRYWOOD, THE MCLEAN, VIRGINIA, ESTATE OF HER MOTHER JANET AND STEPFATHER HUGH AUCHINCLOSS.

PREVIOUS SPREAD ON AUGUST 15, 1942, JACKIE PARTICIPATED IN THE EAST HAMPTON TERCENTENARY CELEBRATION DRIVING A GOVERNESS CART, USED FOR TAKING CHILDREN ON LITTLE JAUNTS.

efforts were directed toward preparing her mare to pull the fifty-year-old sleigh at Miss Porter's. At one point she tied an old metal trash can filled with rocks to the end of the harness, to help with the training. It worked, and eventually Jackie bought her own old ragtop buggy for outings up and down the country lanes.

Her roommate, Nancy Tuckerman, known as Tucky, also shared a love of riding. She would become a lifelong friend, serving as her social secretary at the White House and faithful right hand until Jackie's death. When the two snuck out to ride bareback and Nancy fell off, hurting her arm, Jackie did what many teenagers would do to avoid getting caught. She fabricated a story to get herself and Tucky off the hook.

Jackie's father made the trip from New York to Farmington on the weekends to watch Jackie compete in the school horse shows. When her mare injured a hind leg, he paid for her care, rehabilitation, and rubdowns.

When Danseuse died at the age of twenty, Jackie put together a memory book of photos, notes, and poems. She called her "Donny" a lady, describing her elegant trot and writing: "There was a soft, pink spot at the end of her nose, and she would snuffle softly when she knew you had an apple for her."

After graduating from Farmington, seventeen-year-old Jackie moved into a new phase of her life. She'd experienced loss and pain on numerous levels as a child and adolescent. As a young woman heading off to Vassar, her life became more lighthearted and fun. Her social life began to spin as she stepped into society, but it would not be without a few bumps.

The debutante season in the summer of 1947 was kicked off in Newport with a tea at Hammersmith Farm and a small dance at Newport's Clambake Club. Jackie looked ravishing; it was the summer of her eighteenth birthday. There was just one hitch . . . her father had not been invited. It was not the last time her mother schemed to banish Black Jack from significant family functions.

Gay Estin, a regular rider in today's Virginia horse country, had just graduated from Garrison Forest girl's boarding school in Maryland and was a debutante the same year as Jackie. She also went on to Vassar. They remained in the same horse and social sphere throughout their lives. "Most of the parties were during Christmas vacation," she recalled. "You had two or three parties in a night to go to. Plus tea dances, all that stuff. It was wild. It was fun." Gay, Jackie, and fifty other gorgeous young women wearing the traditional white gown and elbow length gloves formally came out at the Autumn Ball in Tuxedo Park and the Junior Assembly Ball in Manhattan.

By the end of the social season, Jackie was crowned the Debutante of the Year by Igor Cassini, writing under the pen name of Cholly Knickerbocker in the *New York Journal-American*. His brother, Oleg Cassini, would later be her principal couturier when Jackie became First Lady.

At Vassar, Jackie continued her equestrian pursuits. She rode out hunting with classmates Annette Shelden and Betty Hadden with the Rombout Hunt in Dutchess County, New York. Ted Freudy, who followed many of the major horse events in the northeast, captured them in a photograph. The hunt, established in 1929, covers one hundred square miles. Jackie frequently walked around the campus in her riding clothes. And at least one male suitor noted that she talked mostly about animals. She also spent a year in France, perfecting her language skills, and she traveled throughout Europe on the grand tour. In order to be near her horses at Merrywood, she completed her last year of college at George Washington University in Washington, D.C., earning a degree in French Literature.

After winning and later declining an internship with *Vogue* magazine in Paris, Jackie, then twenty-two, sailed to Europe on the Queen Elizabeth in the summer of 1951. In the fall, she accepted a job as the "Inquiring Photographer" at the now defunct *Washington Times-Herald* newspaper for $56.75 a week. Dressmaker Mini Rhea wrote, "She was interested in the lives of all people and curious to fathom their inner impulses." She interviewed the high and the mighty in the nation's capital, including Richard M. Nixon and John F. Kennedy, long before they were introduced in a social setting. And she would also conduct whimsical interviews, such as asking her horsey friends at the Middleburg Hunter Trials, "What do you like best about foxhunting?" Several of those friends continued to ride with her throughout her life.

Jackie made her way to the horse country whenever possible. But her visit in the autumn of 1951 was not as pleasant as her previous trip as the "Inquiring Photographer." This time Jackie was out riding with the Piedmont Hunt in Virginia and her horse stepped in a hole. She took her first serious spill from a horse, falling headfirst onto the rock-hard frozen ground. She was knocked unconscious and was already turning blue before being resuscitated by a fellow

OPPOSITE IN THE FALL OF 1950 JACKIE RODE WITH THE ROMBOUT HUNT WITH VASSAR CLASSMATES ANNETTE SHELDEN AND BETTY HADDEN IN DUTCHESS COUNTY, NEW YORK.

rider. Her father begged her to stop hunting. Of course, the tumble did not faze her a bit.

The following May her life took a turn when she was formally introduced to a bright, handsome young congressman from Massachusetts, John F. Kennedy. They began to see each other on a regular basis, making the rounds of parties in Georgetown. By the fall of that year, Jackie and Jack Kennedy were considered a serious couple.

In May 1952, Jackie sailed to England to cover the coronation of Queen Elizabeth II for the *Times-Herald*. While on board ship, she wrote a delightful story about all the dogs making the crossing. When she returned, Jack Kennedy was waiting at the dock. He gave her an emerald-and-diamond engagement ring.

The little girl who loved her ponies was now an alluring young woman. And at twenty-three years old, she still found time for her horses. A quiet moment in a vacant field petting her charges somehow enabled her to cope with life's difficult decisions and crossroads.

Horse Talk

BLANK: Failure to find a fox in a covert is to draw blank. Failure to find a fox all day is to have a blank day.

BREAKFAST: Meal served by a host after a hunt, either buffet or sit-down.

BUTTON: The hunt button is a black or brass button with the hunt's distinctive logo engraved on it. This is worn only at the invitation of the Master.

CANTER: A well controlled three beat gait.

CAPPING FEE: Paid by non-members to ride with the field. Usually limited to two or three visits before a membership application is expected. Also, a rider's hard hat.

COFFEE HOUSING: Distracting field chitchat while others are listening for hounds.

CHARLES: Respectful name for the fox. Also known as Charlie, gentleman Charles, Charles James, the old gentleman, Reynard, varmint, Uncle Remus.

COLORS: Distinctive hunt livery worn by members at the invitations of a Master.

COOP: Chicken coop. An inviting, three-foot high (or more), A-frame, roof-like jump.

COUNTRY: The hunt's general territory as registered with the Master Fox Hounds Association.

COVERT: (cover) Woods or dense growth where a fox may be found.

CROP: The stick part of a hunting whip, not the whole assembly.

CUBBING: Pre-season hunting that teaches cubs to run from the pack and teaches puppies to hunt with the pack. Also, cub hunting.

EARTH: Where a fox goes to ground for safety, usually a den or kennel.

EX-MFH: Former master of foxhounds.

FIXTURE: Time and place of a meet. Also, a regular location for a meet.

FIXTURE CARD: Card sent to members and individuals invited to hunt. Lists dates, places, and times of meets.

FULL CRY: Sound of many hounds hunting hot and heavy as a pack.

GONE AWAY: Fox has left the covert, the chase is on.

GO TO GROUND: When the fox escapes into a hole in the ground.

HAND: A form of measurement equal to four inches, the horse is measured from top of witheres to the ground.

HEADS UP: Hounds raise their heads and lose the scent. A sin if caused by riders.

HOUND: Canine used for hunting by scent.

CONTINUED

HUNTSMAN: Individual who hunts the hounds.

JOINT MASTERS: Two or more masters who share responsibilities for hunt operations in one hunting club.

LIVERY: Attire of the professional staff. Usually particular to a hunt.

MFH: Master of foxhounds. Individual in charge of hunt operations in fields and kennels.

MEET: Assembling of a hunt on a given day. See Fixture.

MOVE OFF: Hounds, staff, and field head out to begin the hunt.

OVERRIDE: To press hounds too closely, especially at a check. Also, to get in front of a field master during run. Both are bad manners.

OXER: A wide jump consisting of two parts, jumped as one obstacle, used to test the horse's ability to jump a spread fence.

PIE: A cream or fawn hound color.

BADGER PIE: Legs, head, belly, and tail of cream while ears and back shade into black with lighter badger-colored hair tips. Hare-pie: similar, but hairs shade to brown, ends are a lighter hare color.

PINK: The red/scarlet coat with white breeches ensemble, not the color of the coat. Named after the original tailor from London, Mr. Pinque.

POINT-TO-POINT: Annual fund-raising horse races sponsored by the hunt, not sanctioned by the National Steeplechase Association and not to be confused with the Steeplechase Races.

RATCATCHER: Informal hunting attire.

RIOT: When hounds chase anything they shouldn't.

SCOPEY: A horse with a great deal of depth and jumping ability.

STERN: Hound's tail.

STIRRUP CUP: Libation served to mounted followers before they move off.

TAILGATE: Informal snacks after a hunt.

TALLY HO: A fox has been viewed.

THE DISTANCE: The ideal point of takeoff in front of the jump.

TUCKED UP: A horse is drawn inward in the flanks, usually after a race or hunting, following a long run and after sweating profusely.

USET: United States Equestrian Team.

WHIPPER-IN: Staff who assists the huntsman with hounds, usually going out ahead to watch for a fox going away or to keep hounds off a highway.

WARE!: Beware! Alert used with hound, wire, hole, low bridge, bees, deer, hare, riot, etc., as in "Ware hound."

ABOVE IN THIS EVENT AT THE SMITHTOWN HORSE SHOW ON AUGUST 30, 1941, JACKIE IS RIDING DANSEUSE WITH A DOUBLE BRIDLE, WHICH HAS TWO BITS AND TWO REINS.

SANCTUARY

1953-1963

JACQUELINE BOUVIER SOUGHT TRANQUILITY AS HER WHIRLWIND LIFE IN THE PUBLIC EYE BEGAN. DINNERS IN GEORGETOWN WITH

the handsome Jack Kennedy, now a senator, would be followed by tranquil weekends out riding in the Virginia countryside.

Three months later, on September 12, 1953, several thousand people stood outside St. Mary's Church in Newport when Jacqueline Bouvier married John Fitzgerald Kennedy. The lavish event included twenty-six ushers and bridesmaids, seven hundred guests at the wedding, and hundreds more for the reception at Hammersmith Farm. The Republic of Niger even created a stamp in honor of the occasion. Photos of the glittering day were beamed around the world. It was the beginning of Jackie's arduous and often vexing relationship with photographers.

Beneath the joy, the day stirred a multitude of momentous emotions in Jackie. After spending several days leading up to the wedding in Newport, her father was denied the honor of escorting her up the aisle. Whether he simply was ostracized or had hit the bottle

too hard will never be clear. Black Jack was persona non grata, and struggling through the memory of her wedding day without her beloved father produced lifelong hurt. Jack Bouvier died of liver cancer four years later.

When H. Purcell's "Trumpet Voluntary" wedding processional finally began Hugh D. Auchincloss held out his arm for his stepdaughter. Pope Pius XII sent his blessing for the ceremony, which was conducted by Archbishop Richard Cushing of Boston.

After a honeymoon in Acapulco, Jackie and Jack settled into married life. Like many newlyweds, their differences surfaced: His appetite leaned toward all-American square meals of meat and potatoes, her preferences included *anything* French. The Bouvier family favored the Republican party, yet Jackie immediately adopted her husband's political persuasion. She reluctantly accepted his social preference for large gatherings. And besides his well-documented, insatiable hunger for other women, there was another very important fact horse-loving Jackie didn't know when they were married.

He was allergic to animal fur.

The attractive young Kennedys became a family with the birth of Caroline in 1957. John Jr. was born between the 1960 presidential election and the inauguration in January 1961. As Jackie prepared to relinquish her anonymity and become First Lady, a January 1961 cover story in *Time* magazine predicted, "She will live as a cynosure. Her every public act will cause comment, her chance remarks will raise controversy, and the way she raises her children will bring criticism."

"There's no question that the First Lady's main form of relaxing from the tensions of her job was riding," noted Letitia Baldrige, who referred to life at the White House as a frenetic goldfish bowl. "Riding was how she could get away from everything and everybody."

By the beginning of January, Jackie had already been flooded with three hundred appearance requests.

Before they moved into the White House, Jackie contacted her friends Eve and Paul Fout in Middleburg. The lush horse country of Virginia provided the opportunity for seclusion just forty-two miles west—a half-hour helicopter hop away. The Fouts spent many memorable hours with the Kennedys at quiet dinners in the country and intimate gatherings at the White House.

Middleburg and the surrounding hamlets were home to wealthy old Virginia families such as the Randolphs and the Dulanys. Bunny and Paul Mellon lived ten miles farther west in Upperville. Besides the Old Virginia money, there were a few lawyers and retired ambassadors scattered about. It was home at one time to such national heroes as generals Billy Mitchell and George Patton—both horse lovers and fox hunters.

In between the massive farms, at ragged unmarked dirt crossroads called "Frogtown" and "Skinkertown," in true southern style, the area's black working class lived in humble clapboard buildings. Some of these places didn't even have running water. The president's valet, George Thomas, was from nearby Berryville. The explosive civil rights movement had not yet reached this enclave. Still, the backbone of the region consisted of gentlemen and working farmers—men who grew hay, raised sleek horses, and sold cattle at the local auction.

Jackie began searching for a weekend retreat while recuperating from the birth of her son John. She and Jack ventured out to Middleburg one weekend after the election. Then she combed through photos of various properties. On the recommendation of friend and artist William Walton, the Kennedys signed a lease sight-unseen with widow Gladys Tartiere for the 300-acre Glen-Ora.

Paul Fout stepped in as liaison. First, numerous security measures had to be taken at the circa 1780 estate. He coordinated logistics with workmen in the area, and attended to permits and payments. Locals say it looked like an armory as the Secret Service swooped in with communications equipment. In the process of installing wiretaps in the basement, ages old (empty) whiskey barrels were discovered along with mason jars filled with fermented brandied peaches.

Guard stations were set up and a helicopter site was cleared with illumination for night landings. Telephone cables, including the always-available hot line for the president, were added. A secret communications vault was dug under the five-stall stable.

The Kennedys' helicopter, known as a white cap, touched down for their first weekend in the country on February 11, 1961. A hoard of reporters followed the entourage and invaded the once quiet village, which was just recovering from a snowstorm.

The media mob wedged into the creaky second floor of the circa 1728 Red Fox Inn for a briefing from Press Secretary Pierre Salinger. He reported the president

OPPOSITE JACKIE AT GLEN-ORA WITH JFK AND HER SISTER LEE, 1962.

was reading a book by the fire and had a briefcase of papers to work on during the weekend. He informed those gathered, "The president has leased this country place to spend weekends of relaxation and privacy with his family. After today, any news items of Glen-Ora will be released from the White House, not Middleburg." He also let it be known there would be no interviews with the First Lady during her stays in Middleburg. Later, reporters bellied up to the Red Fox bar downstairs, a pine paneled tap-room named "Noble Beveridge" after its former owner. (Beveridge was also the first owner of Glen-Ora.) The hardworking, hard-drinking city reporters were miffed that they could not buy a drink in the then-dry state of Virginia, especially given the name of the room.

The onslaught of journalists eventually subsided, but not for the lack of a stiff drink. When they figured no news would be coming out of Middleburg, they returned to Washington, fifty miles away. One Teletype machine was kept up and pumping at the Red Fox just in case. From time to time, an occasional stray photographer could be spotted from a mile away strolling the brick sidewalks, easily identified sporting new country clothes and boots.

Located less than two miles from the main intersection of the village, Glen-Ora was first surveyed by George Washington in 1747. Long before the Kennedy's took up residence, it was a 1,200-acre working farm, with slave quarters, a smokehouse, an ice cellar, and a six-hole privy, which still stands. (When indoor plumbing was installed at the beginning of the 1900s, it was believed to be one of the first houses in Middleburg with such a modern convenience, not to mention a claw-foot bathtub.)

Accessible by an isolated dirt lane lined with Civil War era dry stone walls, the property also boasted several cottages, a swimming pool, and terraced gardens. Tartiere had been living in Chicago, and the ochre color stucco covered main house was in need of refurbishing inside and out. This would later cause a flap when the fine print of the lease revealed that any changes made on the property had to be restored back to their original condition, no matter what.

Jackie Kennedy gave society decorator Sister Parish three weeks and carte blanche to repaint, wallpaper, and redo the six-bedroom house. Tartiere's fancy French antiques from former homes in Paris and Fountainbleau were placed in storage, and the Kennedy's comfortable family furnishings from Georgetown were installed. Pink slipcovers and flowered chintz (the English country, shabby chic look still popular today) were requisitioned. Wall-to-wall carpets were laid down in the upstairs bedrooms. The only unchanged room in the mansion was a room set aside for the president. A den near the central hall provided a retreat for him to read and watch television on an oversized screen.

Jackie considered Glen-Ora her sanctuary, but it was an expensive sanctuary. The final $10,000 tab— a personal expense, not reimbursed by the government—was the first of many financial flash points between Jackie and the president. (One month in 1963, her expenses for the children were $300 and the animal expenses were $1,500. This included feed, straw, liniment, and a new horse vacuum cleaner.)

Page Allen, several years older than Caroline, recalled, "Apparently [Jackie] took a shine to me. And so they called me one day and invited me to come over and they sent a van for my pony and we rode and went in the house and played. Caroline wanted me to be her pony and her mother and father were in there, too. I think her mother might have been reading. It was a cold winter day and there was a fire going and JFK was in the wing chair. Later we had dinner and it was just the children and I and Maude Shaw, the nanny or nurse or whatever you call her. Jackie came through a couple of times and John was making a mess, pouring milk into his food and mixing it all around. He was tiny, maybe two, just a little thing. Later on, on their way back to Washington, they took me home in a caravan of limos."

The Fouts arranged to supply the horses and ponies to the first family. For Jackie, it was a dark brown hunter she named Bit O' Irish in honor of her husband's ancestry. For Caroline, it would be one of the most special ponies in all the land. His name was Macaroni.

Eve Fout put a phone call into Barney Brittle, a local horse trainer and trader. He still remembered the conversation some forty years later. They were looking for a "push button" pony, a safe, sound, and well-trained mount. His fat little roan pony, Macaroni, had taught his children Skip, Gould, and Shawn to ride.

Macaroni loved to eat and was forever intent on polishing off any bit of fresh grass he could find. He was as wide as an easy chair. When tacked up for riding, his bridle included a special "checking" device that prevented him from putting his head down to eat. If a little rider was holding onto the reins and the pony put his head down, he could possibly pull the rider out of the

OPPOSITE CAROLINE ON MACARONI AND GOULD BRITTLE ON TEX TROT ACROSS THE WHITE HOUSE LAWN ON MARCH 17, 1962.

saddle. His brownish color was highlighted with white spots in whimsical places on his side and rump. Fat and contented, he looked like a big bear with four white legs.

Eve Fout told Brittle she was looking for a pony for one of her friends. "Well, we might consider selling him," Brittle said. "Where's he going?" He never bothered to ask who Eve's friend was; it didn't matter, as long as the pony was going to a good home. He loaded Macaroni in the back of his horse trailer and took him on the five or six mile ride to Glen-Ora to meet his new rider: Caroline Kennedy.

Sometime later in the spring, Brittle received another memorable phone call.

"Mr. Brittle? It's Mrs. Kennedy," Jackie half-whispered in a breathy voice. She continued before he had a chance to say anything. "You'll never guess what happened. Caroline got into my nail polish and she painted Macaroni's hooves red."

It would be the first of many phone calls from the First Lady to Brittle, who over the next two and one-half years would serve as trainer, coach, and horse

OPPOSITE MAY 26, 1962: CAROLINE KENNEDY, LED BY HER MOTHER, WINS HER FIRST BLUE RIBBON AT THE APPLE BARREL SHOW IN MIDDLEBURG.

confidante. They traveled to New York City to her favorite horse show at Madison Square Garden, taking his children and hers. They went to a series of local pony club events called the Apple Barrel Pony Shows, and eventually Jackie even dropped the title Mr. Brittle and called him Barney.

Jackie was now taking her "weekends" in the country from Thursday to Tuesday. The newspapers chronicled her comings and goings. She chose not to attend an event for the National Council of Negro Women. She passed up the Congressional Wives' Prayer Breakfast. She avoided particular official events, especially ones where she had to stand in a mind-numbing receiving line and shake hands. If her husband could make it to Glen-Ora. . .fine. And, if for whatever reason—be it presidential or extramarital—he could not. . .well that was fine, too. Once again, the horses offered a much-cherished diversion. And while it eventually became no state

secret, close friend Paul Fout confirms, "He really lived his own life and she did her own thing."

Her efforts to introduce her daughter into the wonderful world of horses were succeeding. Caroline won her first blue ribbon at the Apple Barrel Pony Show at the home of Bev and Dr. Bob "Doc" McConnell on May 26, 1962.

The events were named as such: Apple Dumplins for the lead line, Sour Apples were the little riders who could walk and trot, and the Green Apples were riders who could jump on their own. Jackie would lead Caroline around the ring. She sat on the ground chatting with all the other parents and helped serve lemonade.

Just as the *East Hampton Star* once recorded the winnings of young Jackie, this time the *Washington Star* reported Caroline's day at the horse show in an eerie déjà vu with a full page of photos. Under the headline "No Sour Apples for

CAROLINE ON MACARONI WITH HER FIRST BLUE RIBBON, MAY 26, 1962, IN MIDDLEBURG.

Caroline," Dolores Phillips reported the First Lady coached her daughter just like "any dedicated pony club mother." Jackie's demeanor in giving riding instruction to her own daughter was much kinder and gentler than the stern admonitions she'd received from her own mother.

"Favoritism, on the pony level, was way down at the bottom of the barrel since Caroline's seat and hands and her handling of Macaroni were just plain better than her competitors," the reporter wrote. "She was awarded not just the lovely, fluttery blue ribbon, but a silver horseshoe pin with a horse head in the middle. Like any other pony club mother, Mrs. Kennedy was more excited than Caroline. Grandmother Auchincloss watched from the rail and lunched, with the first family, under the trees during intermission."

Jackie and her sister Lee embarked on a much-publicized trip to India at the suggestion of John Kenneth Galbraith, the U.S. ambassador there. A hairdresser, maid, press secretary, and twenty-four security guards accompanied them. They took sixty-four pieces of luggage.

OPPOSITE JACKIE TAKES CAROLINE IN THE LEADLINE CLASS AT THE APPLE BARREL PONY SHOW NEAR MIDDLEBURG ON MAY 27, 1961.

They stayed at the Pink Palace as guests of the maharajah and maharani of Jaipur. They attended a polo match. Jackie also went riding and jumped the horse beautifully, but one of the Indian officers along with her was thrown off his horse.

Jackie and Lee were photographed at the Amber Palace riding Bibia, a thirty-five-year-old elephant. His false wooden tusks were painted and decorated for the festivities. They sat on a high gold seat called a howdah. Jackie thought it was great fun. She brought back fabrics and costumes for the children.

Some of the fabrics were put to good use when Caroline reprised her mother's 1939 performance in the fancy dress class at a horse show. Shawn Brittle, dragging a faux tiger skin, accompanied her. They were entered as "Best Tiger Killers." Jackie later sent photographer Howard Allen, who took a shot of

OPPOSITE JUNE 27, 1962: AT THE PLAINS COMMUNITY LEAGUE HORSE SHOW, CAROLINE KENNEDY RODE IN THE COSTUME CLASS JUST AS HER MOTHER HAD MANY YEARS BEFORE.

For Howard Allen — who took this — my favorite picture
with all good wishes always
Jacqueline Kennedy

December 25, 1962

Caroline in her costume, his photo framed, with a note: "For Howard Allen, who took this—my favorite picture. With all good wishes always, Jacqueline Kennedy."

Allen, a lifelong resident of the area, had the inside advantage as both a parent and an accomplished photographer, capturing the first family on many occasions. "I could go out in the ring, and after a while she knew I wouldn't sell [the photos] to the magazines. She could be herself," he said.

Thanks to that rare trust, he was invited out to Glen-Ora one morning on November 19, 1962, where he took one of the most enchanting shots of Jackie and her children. "She called on a Sunday and asked if I could come over at 9 A.M. on Monday. She wanted to take a photo with the children. Of course, when I got there she wasn't ready."

Allen dutifully waited until groom David Lloyd brought the horses out and Jackie mounted up. She held John Jr., who was still too little to sit on a pony

alone, in front of her on the saddle. Caroline rode along beside her, and they walked up and down the country lane as he snapped away. "I'm just sorry I didn't have a zoom lens in those days," Allen said.

As the photo session drew to a close, the helicopter began warming up about ten yards away. The president rushed out of the house to get back to work. "He was just about to take off and someone from the Secret Service comes out of the house with a briefcase waving his arms," Allen remembered. "He hands him the briefcase just at they take off. And all I could think of was 'There goes another absent-minded husband.'"

The film was processed and sent off to Washington. "She didn't want anyone to know how or where they were taken," he recalled. "It was Caroline and John's birthday the next week." She paid him four dollars for an 8 x 10 print, which was released by the White House and "printed around the world."

While the first family commuted to Washington by helicopter, Macaroni was traveling back and forth in a horse trailer. When he was in Middleburg, they caught him tromping all over the putting green Jackie had installed for Jack to perfect his stroke. While in D.C., the adorable pony was able to munch on White House grass. One day, the president looked up and there was Macaroni right outside the oval office. He was devouring his gourmet lunch of red roses faster than Bunny Mellon could replant the famous rose garden.

Because all the tourists at 1600 Pennsylvania Avenue were constantly feeding him through the fence, chicken wire had to be installed so he couldn't get extra treats. Then, in addition to the swing sets, slides, tree house, and trampoline for the children, Macaroni needed a new stable. A potting shed was soon converted into a barn.

The little round pony named Macaroni became such a White House favorite, the Marine Corps band even performed an original song in his honor, entitled "My Pony Macaroni." Composed by Bill Snyder, it was, appropriately, a foxtrot. The song also was recorded on several 45 rpm discs. Decca Records produced one version conducted by Dick Jacobs, performed by Snyder and his orchestra. A second Golden Record rendition for children was recorded as a collaboration between The Sandpipers and Jim Timmens and his Orchestra.

Macaroni received thousands of fan letters. Jackie taught him to pull a sleigh, just as she had done with Danseuse while at boarding school. She loaded up Caroline and some of her nursery school friends for a ride one day. The Kennedys' personal Christmas card in 1961 showed Jackie and the children in the snow on the south lawn, with Macaroni pulling them in an antique sleigh.

PREVIOUS SPREADS NOVEMBER 19, 1962: AT GLEN-ORA, JACKIE KENNEDY HOLDS JOHN JR. WHILE RIDING SARDAR, JOINED BY CAROLINE ON MACARONI.

OPPOSITE PRESIDENT KENNEDY TAKES A BREAK FROM THE OVAL OFFICE WITH CAROLINE AND MACARONI, JUNE 22, 1962. NANNY MAUDE SHAW AND ANOTHER PONY ARE IN THE BACKGROUND.

When Shabanou Farah Diba of Iran came for a White House visit one afternoon, Macaroni put in an appearance on the front driveway just off Pennsylvania Avenue. Jackie, in a wool suit and heels, led him around. The president, sitting at his famous Resolute Desk in the Oval Office, spotted Caroline, whom he frequently called Buttons, and took a few moments from his busy schedule to watch her ride around.

Jackie's love of horses and riding—a sport associated with elitism and exclusivity in the minds of many Americans—caused concerns within the West Wing. "The buzz word was Middleburg," said Nancy Hogan Dutton. She worked on the coveted first floor as an administrative aide to Fred Dutton, one of nine special assistants to the president. Anytime word got out that Jackie was going to Middleburg, the tiny horsey hamlet also conjured up images of snobbery.

OPPOSITE MACARONI HAD THE RUN OF THE WHITE HOUSE GROUNDS, JUNE 22, 1962.

"[JFK] had won the election by the slimmest of margins and this was an elitist sport. Everybody kept saying, 'Keep her out of Middleburg.' They were constantly wringing their hands over it. And it certainly wouldn't look good for the president's re-election."

Fred Dutton received a memo from the Department of Agriculture. There was a rumor President Bourguiba of Tunisia was sending a horse to President Kennedy. The information came via a representative of Air France in New York, who had been told of it by a vet at the quarantine station.

Dutton walked a fine line. Everyone knew of Jackie's love of horses, as well as her desire to maintain a certain level of aloofness from White House politics. "We had to be respectful of her detachment from governmental concerns. I don't think anyone in the early part of the Kennedy White House years wanted to cross Jackie." On the other hand, he commented, "From the view inside, we thought Mrs.

Kennedy's horses were pretty aristocratic and didn't play well with Joe Sixpack."

Dutton shot off a quick memo to warn of possible embarrassment. On April 3, 1961, he wrote: "It has been suggested that either the State Department or the Animal Inspection and Quarantine Division of the Agriculture Department should take immediate steps to contact the Tunisian Government or their veterinary officials and outline import requirements if such a shipment is to take place."

Fortunately for this diplomatic quandary, it seems there had been an outbreak of African horse sickness in that region of the world. Horses from Egypt and Jordan had already been refused entry into the U.S. after reacting positive to a test for the disease. A report on the sickness from the Armed Forces Institute of Pathology at Walter Reed Army Medical Center estimated 150,000

PREVIOUS SPREAD JUNE 22, 1962: JFK HELPS CAROLINE ADJUST HER STIRRUPS.

OPPOSITE MARCH 30, 1962: CAROLINE AND MACARONI (WITH AN UNIDENTIFIED SECRET SERVICE AGENT) TAKE A WALK ON THE WHITE HOUSE LAWN.

horses, mules, and donkeys had recently died in the eastern Mediterranean area and Southeast Asia. If contacted, the mortality rate was estimated at ninety percent. Needless to say, the horse was never shipped, and any chance of an equine epidemic (not to mention a difficult political situation) was averted.

There were no diplomatic issues involved when Vice President Lyndon B. Johnson gave Macaroni a new friend in the form of a yearling Galiceno horse. (He also gave Jackie four cows to decorate the pastures at Glen-Ora. They multiplied quickly to four cows plus three calves and a bull.)

The original Galiceno Horse Breeders' registration forms for the buckskin horse record his name as Little John. He was later renamed Tex, perhaps because he came from John B. Connally, who bred the horse at his ranch in Floresville, Texas. Connally had served as Johnson's congressional and senate campaign manager before Kennedy named him as secretary of the Navy in '61. He was elected governor of Texas in 1962 and was wounded himself while riding in the car in Dallas when the president was assassinated on November 22, 1963.

OPPOSITE JUNE 22, 1962: THE PRESIDENT HEADS BACK TO WORK AFTER WATCHING CAROLINE GO FOR A RIDE ON MACARONI.

"He is not saddle broken, and ponies of this type are not broken to ride until they are eighteen months old, which in the case of Tex will be about September of this year," Johnson wrote in a letter to Jackie.

The breed originated in Galicia, an enchanting section of northwestern Spain. Strong, steady, and smooth, they were the preferred horses of the conquistadors, and it's believed they were brought to North America in 1519, when Cortez invaded Mexico. And while they are noted as social animals, there's no way such a young horse would be at all appropriate for a child. Johnson was aware of this. "Finally, with time, patience and continual work, the pony will be ready for the children," he wrote to Jackie. "The ideal situation would be to have a boy with knowledge of horses work with the pony under the supervision of an experienced horseman."

Barney Brittle, who was called to take over the training of Tex, remembered that the horse was "right rough. When Johnson sent the pony from Texas nobody could do anything with it. We thought he was a desert horse from Mexico and a bit inbred." Brittle's son Skip took over riding the horse.

When Johnson asked Jackie how Tex was doing, she called Brittle and asked him to bring Tex to town. Brittle pulled his kids out of school one day, loaded up, and went to the White House.

"I had a dirty Nash station wagon, and I drove right in and parked right behind the car that took the president," he recalled. "Jack left a meeting, and Johnson was there and Senator Anderson and a few from the agricultural committee. And oh, Lynda Bird—she was Miss Busybody." As Lynda Bird asked questions about the horse, Skip rode Tex and Caroline got on Macaroni, and they all went trotting on the White House lawn.

The Kennedys received offers of gift ponies from all over the world. Admirer Carl R. De Pasquale of Stauton,

OPPOSITE LYNDA BIRD JOHNSON, THE FIRST LADY, PRESIDENT KENNEDY, VICE PRESIDENT LYNDON JOHNSON, AND CAROLINE ADMIRE THE NEW PONY TEX, RIDDEN BY YOUNG GOULD BRITTLE, ON MAY 17, 1962.

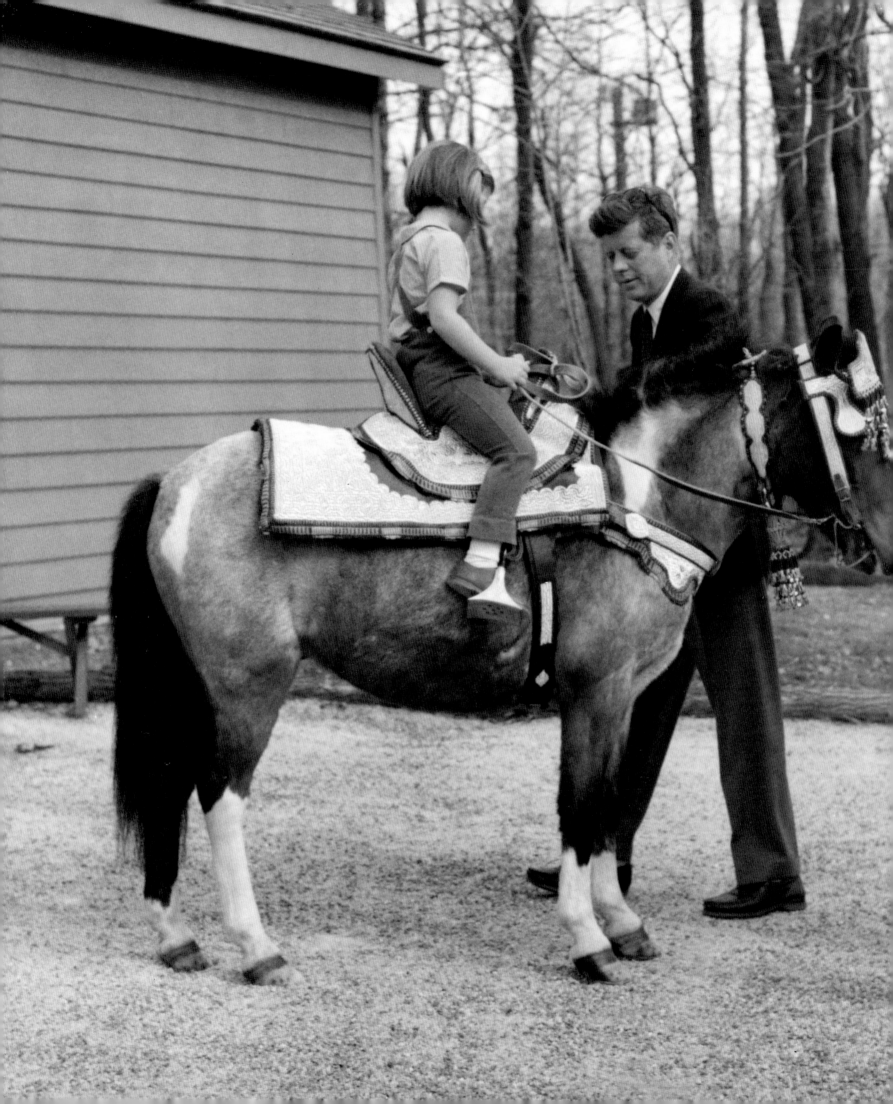

Kentucky, wrote a letter. He wanted to present a Shetland pony called Pasta e Faggiole.

"Your excellency, I have the most fondest admiration for you as our President, a gentleman, and a scholar, and your charming little family as a whole, and even though I am a poor man, I would truly consider it an honor for you to accept the little pony as a gift for your little girl Caroline in return for a personally autographed portrait of you and your charming little family."

JFK's personal secretary, Evelyn Lincoln, graciously replied, "Much as he appreciates your thoughtful offer, the President prefers not to take advantage of your generosity, particularly since there are already two ponies available for the childrens' enjoyment." She concluded with best wishes and enclosed some photographs.

It didn't stop. There were more ponies on the way.

OPPOSITE KING HASSAN II OF MOROCCO SENT A NEW SADDLE AND BRIDLE FOR CAROLINE AND MACARONI, WHICH THE FAMILY TRIES OUT AT CAMP DAVID ON MARCH 31, 1963.

King Hassan II of Morocco had also wanted to present Caroline with another pony. When the thirty-three-year-old monarch made his first trip outside of Africa, he did not come empty-handed. King Hassan, his sister Princess Lalla Aisha, and their entourage disembarked from an antique railcar onto a red carpet at Union Station in Washington, and they came bearing gifts. For Jackie, he brought a majestic, gold filigree, jewel-encrusted cuff bracelet and wide belt. She wore them with an exquisite ivory silk Oleg Cassini evening gown for a state dinner the next evening. For Caroline, there was a pint-sized, blue and white, hand-tooled leather saddle and bridle for Macaroni. A gray pony, with his mane braided in the traditional Moroccan colors of green and red (just like the bracelet), was left behind in a stable in Rabat.

Letters were also exchanged between Chief of Protocol Angier Biddle Duke and Thomas J. Kiernan, the ambassador of Ireland, to sort through the logistics and diplomatic protocol for accepting two Connemara ponies and two deer from President Eamon de Vlera of Ireland.

The Irish-bred ponies, which were to be shipped from Dublin with a groom, were reported to be small and sturdy and no more than three feet high when full grown. In a memo from Duke to presidential advisor Ken O'Donnell at the White House, Duke wondered if such a gift might trigger even more diplomatic quagmires, with other dignitaries desiring "to press similar animal gifts on the president for his children and our defenses would be that much weaker."

The offer was at first declined, noting a White House policy of only accepting gifts of animals during a visit to a foreign country, when the gift was offered by a head of state. Eventually, however, these criteria were met when President Kennedy paid an emotional visit to Ireland.

OPPOSITE AT CAMP DAVID ON MARCH 31, 1963 JACKIE HELPS
MAKE ADJUSTMENTS TO MACARONI'S NEW BRIDLE.

97

The chief of protocol responded to Ambassador Kiernan, "I took the liberty of taking the matter up with Ambassador McCloskey, and he asked me to tell you that he had talked with President Kennedy recently, and that it was the President's understanding that he would be most delighted to receive one Connemara pony and two deer, the latter for the White House lawn." With that, Leprechaun joined the ever-growing stable of ponies.

The animal menagerie at the White House was multiplying. There was Charley, a wirehaired Welsh terrier given to Caroline by her grandfather Joseph P. Kennedy, a gray Russian wolfhound named Wolf, and two hamsters named Debbie and Billie. One hamster drowned in the president's bathtub and the other went missing for two days. Funeral plans were underway when the tiny animal was discovered sleeping on the soft carpet in the president's dressing room.

J. B. West served six first ladies. In his 1973 book *Upstairs at the White House,* he wrote, "I would find myself dealing with Empire tables and rabbit cages; housing maharajahs and ponies; steaming down the Potomac and wearing

OPPOSITE SEPTEMBER 30, 1963: JOHN JR. WAS MORE AMUSED BY HIS TOY AIRPLANE THAN THE NEW PONY, LEPRECHAUN, A GIFT FROM PRESIDENT EAMON DE VALERA OF IRELAND.

disguises; and thoroughly enjoying the most creative and challenging work to which the chief usher had ever been put."

Add a tank full of goldfish, a canary named Robin, two parakeets named Bluebell and Marybelle and several ducks to the mix. Tom Kitten did not get on too well with all the others and was given to Jackie's assistant Mary Gallagher; the children visited him several times. Pushinka, an offspring of the Russian Sputnik 5 canine astronaut, Strelka, was a gift from Premier Khruschev. From Germany came Clipper, a German shepherd, who was constantly at Jackie's side. Shannon, a cocker spaniel, was yet another gift from Ireland. And a hutch of gray and white rabbits lived upstairs in the White House nursery school. One was named Zsa-Zsa. Another, Annabelle, gave birth to four bunnies, only to later eat them. It was a perplexing situation to explain to the children.

Romance bloomed among this collection of animals, and Charley and

Pushinka soon produced four puppies, acclaimed as the first-ever Russian-American canines. Butterfly, White Tips, Blackie, and Streaker were later offered as pets to good homes in a White House letter writing contest.

Jackie and Lee toured the Middle East and visited Pakistan. The reception was again staggering, as it had been in India. Balloons floated through the air. Flower petals rained down as they arrived in a convertible in the streets of Karachi. This time they rode a camel, not an elephant. For Jackie, the highlight was a visit to the National Horse and Cattle Show in Lahore.

During her visit the dashing and debonair head of Pakistan, President Ayub Khan, who shared a love of horses with Jackie, presented a horse to her. She immediately accepted, going against advice from the White House. The horse was a resplendent bay gelding called

PREVIOUS SPREAD JFK WITH HIS CHILDREN AND LEPRECHAUN.

OPPOSITE MARCH 23, 1962: THE FIRST LADY TAKES HER FIRST RIDE ON SARDAR ON THE GROUNDS OF THE GOVERNOR'S HOUSE IN LAHORE, PAKISTAN.

Sardar, a name which translates as a military commandant of lofty rank. No sooner had Jackie said yes, and Sardar was winging his way to Washington. She hoped he wouldn't get airsick.

Jackie sent a pleading cable:

Dear Jack,

It seems so rude to Pakistanis to suggest that their beautiful horse has hoof-and-mouth disease when obviously he hasn't a germ in the world.

He is so beautiful and high strung it would be cruel to quarantine him in New York for thirty days. Cannot bear to be parted from him that long as could show him this spring and start schooling him immediately.

Could you not have veterinarian examine him in New York and say he was free from all disease and (have him go straight) to Glen-Ora.

It would be like leaving Lee in quarantine to part with him—especially as he has been so frightened past few days by photographers—and plane trip will upset him.

You can leave tiger cubs in quarantine as they are too ferocious to play with—so warn Caroline. Please get Orville Freeman

OPPOSITE JACKIE FEEDS A FRIEND A CARROT IN PAKISTAN, MARCH 1962.

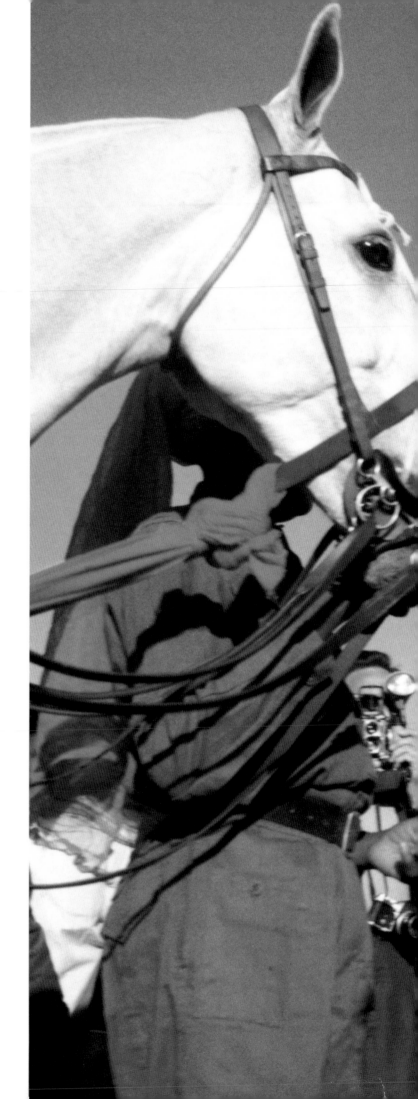

*to let him in quickly—they have Prince
Phillip's polo ponies. Phillip took them
right home—so really think there would be
no criticism and it would be (unfairly)
cruel to animals if you let him (be locked
up in) New York for thirty days. He will
get sick there. All press will say you will
lose ASPCA vote forever if he can't come
straight to Glen-Ora.*

Love Jackie.

The president jokingly replied:

*Dave, Kenny, Ted, Taz, McHugh,
Evelyn, Bob, Dean, and I are doing nothing
but taking care of Sardar. Don't worry.*

All love, Jack

The gift horse caused quite a diplomatic dustup. Letitia Baldrige was called into the Oval Office by the president. "He told me, 'Letitia, you are the only one who can help me. You have got to make a phone call for me.' The president was furious." As damage control for the acceptance of what could be perceived as an inappropriate gift, JFK wanted to find out the value of the horse and then pay the duty. "Or I'll be in trouble," he told her. Kennedy asked Baldrige to call the embassy of Pakistan and determine the value. "I told him I couldn't do that. But he said I was the only one who could," she said. Baldrige's graceful etiquette was already recognized and appreciated.

Baldrige had no option but to make the call. She picked up the phone and asked the White House switchboard to connect her to the ambassador from Pakistan. "I'm so sorry, Mr. Ambassador, to have to ask you this," she began apologetically. "This is so embarrassing. Please forgive me. But I must ask you, how much is the horse worth?"

"That horse is worth nothing," replied the ambassador emphatically. "He's a piece of junk."

Baldrige was speechless. She held her breath. She began to stutter, then she

Eve on Sardar — at his First American Horse Show

For Eve — who can do miracles and make
it all look so easy!
With much love —

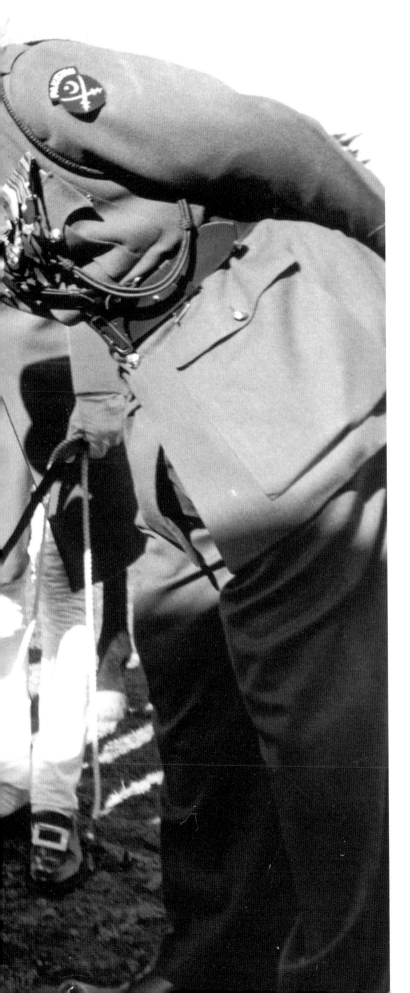

heard the voice on the other end laugh. "He recognized my voice, he threw me off. The White House operator had misunderstood." Baldrige was talking to the ambassador from Afghanistan, not Pakistan. Then, as now, the two countries were at odds, but humor prevailed. The matter was settled, and after a grueling thirty-hour flight, Sardar landed at Fort Myer.

Sardar was immediately sprayed with fungicide, a preventative measure to avoid the possibility of the horse carrying a rare disease into the country. "The horse went berserk," Paul Fout recalled. "The stable sergeant was a vet and they used a fire hose. He handled it well and the sergeant was to be congratulated."

Eve Fout was invited to the official presentation of Sardar. She and Jackie stood outside and looked on as the big horse was led around. They chatted about the way he walked and trotted, his style and carriage. The Pakistani attendants,

dressed in traditional garb, allowed Caroline to pet Sardar. Jackie also received a green leather-bound book, embossed in gold, filled with the details of Sardar's breeding. He was foaled in 1952 by a stallion named Copper Knight.

The Fouts took Sardar back to Middleburg and began working on getting him acclimated. Eve rode him during the week and Jackie rode him on the weekends.

"Jackie just loved the outdoors. I think it was a complete escape. She loved to go hacking on Sardar and all that kind of thing," Eve said. "She was a very good rider. And then she was completely relaxed and, you know, never interfered with the horse." While out riding, Jackie was just one of a large group of horse lovers. There's one story that has floated around Middleburg for years. When someone once asked, "What does Mrs. Kennedy's husband do?" The reply was simply, "He's in politics."

According to Eve, who continues to ride and hunt, along with her work to preserve the wide open spaces in Middleburg, the entire experience for Jackie was "a wonderful way of being with people in a very natural situation. It was a great relaxation. A wonderful way to bring up the children in a relaxed, open situation as well. So in spite of the pressure that was brought on her, you know, she could gain the privacy and the outdoor exercise."

Jackie, whose weight fluctuated between 123 to 133 pounds most of her adult life, enjoyed the exercise, according to her chief of staff. "She stayed in good shape," Baldrige said. "And if she ate something rich, she would exercise it off for three hours or ride a bit longer to burn extra calories."

When President Ayub Khan came to the states in September 1962, he carved out time for a ride with Jackie in Middleburg between diplomatic dinners in Washington and a meeting with Secretary General U. Thant at the

United Nations in New York. They made a quick trip to the country by helicopter. Jackie rode Sardar and Khan rode a horse called Minbreno on loan from Eve Fout. When they finished hacking around Glen-Ora, Khan dismounted, leaned against the fence, and watched as Jackie took Sardar over several jumps.

Sardar fit into Jackie's horse program effortlessly. He was docile when she propped young Caroline up on his back. He hacked in the horse shows confidently. He even adapted to the ladies sidesaddle when Eve Fout entered him in the prestigious Washington International Horse Show, a show that marks the end of major circuit competition and is a fixture on the social circuit in the nation's capital.

The First Lady added sparkle when she stepped in to serve as honorary

PREVIOUS SPREAD JACKIE KENNEDY HAS QUITE A RIDE ON SARDAR IN MIDDLEBURG, SEPTEMBER 1962.

OPPOSITE SEPTEMBER 25, 1962: JACKIE TAKES SARDAR OVER A JUMP WHILE PRESIDENT AYUB KHAN OF PAKISTAN LOOKS ON DURING A BRIEF VISIT TO GLEN-ORA.

chairman of the event, and a new international jumping event, the President's Cup, was inaugurated. The normally drab D.C. Armory was magically transformed into a colorful, sold-out show. Jumping teams from Argentina, Canada, Ireland, Mexico, and the United States were featured. Steinkraus served as captain of the United States Equestrian Team.

Jackie's horse loving sister-in-law, Ethel Skakel Kennedy, made a comeback in the show ring, riding Claude W. Owen's chestnut mare Sky's Pride in the Conformation Hunter Appointments Class during the opening evening performance. Robert Kennedy, then attorney general, and five of their seven children watched from the box, along with Don Wilson, deputy director of the USIA. In the end, Ethel's horse had a rail down, eliminating the possibility of a prize. Their children Kathleen and Joseph rode in the pony hunter classes on another day during the show.

For the grand finale of the six-day competition, Jackie, radiant in a long

OPPOSITE SEPTEMBER 25, 1962: JACKIE BRINGS
SARDAR OUT OF THE STABLES AT GLEN-ORA
TO SHOW HIM TO PRESIDENT AYUB KHAN.

PREVIOUS SPREAD PRESIDENT AYUB KHAN RIDES OUT WITH JACKIE
ON A VISIT TO GLEN-ORA ON SEPTEMBER 25, 1962.

evening gown, stepped into the spotlight to present a silver trophy from Tiffany & Co. to the winner of the President's Cup International Jumping Competition. The Kennedys hosted a black-tie pre-show dinner party at the White House with horse lover Alice Roosevelt Longworth, a well-known socialite and oldest daughter of Theodore Roosevelt, as a guest of honor. Later they all sat in a box with Eunice Shriver, writer Gore Vidal (Jackie's distant relative by marriage), and William Walton (who had arranged the Glen-Ora lease along with Eve and Paul Fout).

While the well-known and well-to-do passed a pleasant evening at the horse show, headlines in the *Washington Star* did not report the results of the events of the show on the front page. Instead, the paper hailed the recent launch of the space booster rocket Saturn, reported tensions in Berlin between Soviet and U.S. forces, and included a note that troops between South Vietnam and Cambodia had exchanged gunfire. The

horse show received minimal coverage in the sports section.

When the president accompanied Jackie to the show, his presence created a commotion, with a "pushing, shoving, neck-craning, cheering melee of horse-fanciers and Kennedy-fanciers," according to an article by Anne Christmas in the *Star* sports section. He slipped out early, and she stayed to present the trophy and blue ribbon to Carlos Damm, an eighteen-year-old rider from Argentina, on his horse Sheriff. The young equestrian collected $500 for his victory.

In 1962 the total prize money was doubled to $2,000, with $1,000 for the winner. Although the Cuban Missile Crisis prevented the First Lady from attending the horse show that year, the President's Cup went on as planned. Kathy Kusner, a member of the United States Equestrian Team, was the eventual winner on the horse Unusual.

OPPOSITE EVE FOUT RODE SARDAR IN THE LADIES SIDESADDLE CLASS AT THE OCTOBER 1961 WASHINGTON INTERNATIONAL HORSE SHOW. THE PRESIDENT AND MRS. KENNEDY WATCHED FROM THEIR BOX WHILE THEY ENTERTAINED GUESTS.

Betty Beale, a society columnist for the *Washington Star*, rebuked Jackie for her absence. In her "Exclusively Yours" column she wrote of the ramifications, "Mrs. Kennedy came in for considerable criticism when she cancelled all engagements that week, including such non-frivolous functions as her reception at the White House for the thirty-eight American poets attending the National Poetry Festival at the Library of Congress; the preview at the National Gallery of Art of the Duke and Duchess of Devonshire's collection of 'Old Master Drawings;' and the Washington International Horse Show, where the First Lady was supposed to present the President's gold cup to the winning rider of the President's Cup class for jumpers . . . Said the critics, 'Mrs. Roosevelt entertained at the White House and made public appearances throughout World War II, and we are not even at war.' Besides, in times of stress, aren't you supposed to keep up appearances of normalcy?"

During this stressful time, Jackie and the president both sought the sanctuary of Glen-Ora. JFK arranged to meet her for a weekend in the country after he had two meetings with the National Security Council early on Saturday morning, November 3, 1962. She went riding and he hit golf balls in a field for a while. It was not the first time the president had escaped to Middleburg for a brief relief from a crisis. During the April 1961 Bay of Pigs invasion, the president went to Middleburg and shot clay pigeons with Paul Fout. He also liked to drive his Thunderbird on the dirt roads. It seems the countryside perhaps had something to offer both Kennedys after all.

For the 1963 Washington International Horse Show, Jackie's mother served as honorary chairman. She entertained Alice Roosevelt Longworth in the president's box, as well as Paul Nitze, the recently appointed secretary of the Navy. Janet Auchincloss looked every bit as glamorous

OPPOSITE JANET BOUVIER AUCHINCLOSS SERVED AS HONORARY CHAIRMAN OF THE 1963 WASHINGTON INTERNATIONAL HORSE SHOW. SHE IS SHOWN HERE WITH UNITED STATES EQUESTRIAN TEAM MEMBER GEORGE MORRIS' HORSE, SINJON.

holding a bouquet of red roses with USET member George Morris' horse, Sinjon, as the last time she had been photographed in the mink coat at the 1934 National Horse Show at Madison Square Garden.

Jackie did not compete in that year, but her eleven-year-old nephew Joseph Kennedy made headlines when he fell off Geronimo twice while preparing for the pony classes. The competition didn't go any smoother for young Joseph, as Geronimo stopped at a fence and was eliminated. Kathleen Kennedy, on her pony Atlas, didn't have any luck either, also missing out on a ribbon. At least one reporter noted they seemed to have fun anyway and spent quite a bit of time at the hot dog stand. Not all Kennedys, it seems, took horse shows as seriously as Jackie had at the same age.

Jackie's adoration of horses was acknowledged each time she made a visit overseas. She accompanied her husband to Vienna where he was meeting with Khrushchev. She visited the 221-year-old Spanish Riding School. The famous white Lipizzan stallions were smuggled from behind enemy lines by General George Patton during World War II. Their performance included the intricate dressage maneuvers of passage, piaffe, and pirouette choreographed to music. The elaborate airs above the ground of the capriole and courbette left caught Jackie spellbound as she watched from the emperor's box.

When Jackie paid a visit to the barracks of the Royal Canadian Mounted Police in Rockcliffe, Ontario, she was photographed nose-to-nose practically kissing one of the horses. Her assistant Mary Gallagher wrote, "Knowing how she loved horses, I knew her smile was sincere."

As usual, Jackie had planned every detail of the trip down to the coordinated color of her suit. The bright scarlet red riding coat worn by the police, as well as certain members of the hunt, is properly referred to as a "pink" coat. It's a commonly held theory that the coat derives its name from the last name of a British tailor. Her friend, designer Oleg Cassini, properly refers to it as "hunting pink."

Many of Jackie's wardrobe choices were influenced by her partiality to the understated equestrian look. Cassini made a coat for her, but she didn't like it because it was too heavy. Her suit in Canada was designed by Pierre Cardin.

Other than a common appreciation of clothing, Cassini said he and Jackie had a special relationship with horses. He served as an instructor of horsemanship in the U.S. Army Calvary in Fort Riley, Kansas, played polo for the Army team and has hunted with more than twenty hunts. They had spent many hours together "talking horses" before he was ultimately chosen as the First Lady's couturier.

"We tried to make a date to ride together and never could make an appointment," he recalled. He even offered to give her a horse, but she said she didn't have room for another one.

When his beloved gray hunter, Galway Ghost, died of a heart attack, she wrote him a sympathy note. Cassini, now in his nineties, still commutes from Oyster Bay Cove on Long Island to his offices in New York City. He continues to ride for pleasure as often as possible and says, "I will always be emotionally involved with horses."

Jackie shared this lifelong passion, said Cassini, and it was "the other side of her life, away from the intrigue of that exalted position. She loved it."

Jackie chose her riding attire with the same attention to detail as she did her evening clothes and afternoon suits. At 35½-26-38, she wore a size ten. From the time Jackie was a little girl, she regularly paid visits to an exclusive equestrian shop at 716 Madison Avenue called M.J. Knoud.

"She had many of her hunting and hacking clothes made to measure," said Dave Wright Jr., whose father owned the establishment. "She and my father became good friends over the years,

and he was proud to include her in his roster of longtime customers." Whenever Jackie came in she'd greet everyone by name, including salesmen Rudy Mitchell and Tom Kittridge, who had been Joseph Kennedy's stable manager in Hyannisport for twenty years. "As she did most everything, she wore riding clothes elegantly and always correct," Wright added.

Correct would entail a black Melton coat made of thirty-two-ounce heavily woven wool. "It's made to repel water," Wright said. The coat was made with the colors of the Piedmont Fox Hounds on the collar as well as the hunt buttons. The colors and the buttons are presented to members of the hunt deemed deserving after several seasons.

William P. Wadsworth, master of the Genesse Valley Hunt from 1932 to 1975, was an authority on attire and hunting etiquette. In his 1987 handbook *Riding to Hounds in America: An Introduction for Foxhunters,* he wrote that enjoyment of the event "comes from the feeling of tradition, and from the spectacle of the people properly and conventionally dressed for the event. You could play the World Series with both teams in slacks and polo shirts, but neither the teams nor the fans would enjoy it quite as much."

Male and female riders wear a long white stock tie, which resembles what some incorrectly call an ascot. The square knot is to be held with a plain gold pin. The tie can double as a tourniquet or sling in case of injury to rider, horse, or hound in the field. A canary yellow vest is worn over the shirt and tie.

Jackie ordered heavy-brushed wool breeches with chamois patches on the inner knee; everything was hand stitched down to the buttonholes. "There was no question about it. That's the way they were to be made, that was the correct way," Wright said.

Jackie's boots were also custom made. Her size eight and a half foot was traced, and her calf, ankles, and length of leg were recorded. For formal hunting she had a pair of black reverse calf boots with patent leather tops. "The reverse calf was to repel briars in the rough country," Wright said. Boot straps and spur rests were added. They were made by Vogel Boots in New York City. Her stepsister, Nina Auchincloss Straight, recalled that when Jackie fell off while out hunting, she informed the paramedics they couldn't cut off her cherished boot to check for broken bones.

She also ordered a pair of plain black calfskin boots without the patent tops, to be worn when riding as a guest of another hunt. "Whenever she hunted elsewhere, she behaved," said Nina, "The coats were plain, no [color on the] collar. There was no pretense on her part. She had a great respect for the traditions of hunting."

For riding cross-country or during the less formal season of hunting known as cubbing, Jackie wore a tweed or houndstooth checked jacket, cotton breeches, and Newmarket boots—part leather and part canvas.

The velvet riding helmet and hard-wool felt derby were ordered from James Lock and Company in London. Again, her head would be measured and a mould was made for the black hats to be finished. Equestrian etiquette calls for hats to be worn squarely, neither on the back of the head or tilted to one side. Ladies are urged to keep their hair inconspicuous and held in a hair net.

Gloves worn are dark brown or black. When it's wet and the reins might slip though the rider's hands, white string gloves are considered proper. Some members of the hunt attach a sandwich case with a flask to the saddle.

For casual riding on the trails, Jackie ordered custom-made chaps from Bevel Saddlery in New Jersey. Peggy Murray took her measurements. "She had really lovely old riding clothes," Murray recalled. "She was fairly frugal; I don't

mean that in a bad way. She never threw money around. The chaps were hand-made by Nancy Stewart, with top grain leather. They were putty color, fairly subdued. She thought it was oh-so-wow, like almost making a statement about herself. Fringe was very big at the time [down the outside leg of the chaps], but she didn't get it. But she did have a needlepoint backing put on the belt in back with JKO." The cost was $175.

The saddle is an important individual choice for a rider, just as it is with a tennis player's racquet or a golfer's clubs. The horse's needs are also a factor; a horse with high withers, for example, might require a saddle with a higher cut. "Because of the length of time spent in the saddle in the hunt field, often as long as three to four hours, it's advisable that the saddle be correctly fitted," explained Gillian DuPont of the Old Habit, a tack shop in Marshall, Virginia. "An ill-fitting saddle can seriously damage a horse's back and will likely result in the poor animal displaying his discomfort, such as bucking, kicking, bolting, and stopping at fences. A saddle which doesn't fit the rider can cause severe back and knee pain and can rub nasty sores on the inside leg. And remember to tighten the girth as you ride off and again at check points. It's undeniably preferable to ride on the horse's back rather than under his belly."

Since Jackie had a number of horses, she owned several different saddles. The Stubben Saddle Company, founded in 1894, manufactures saddles in Stans, Switzerland. With transactions in fifty countries, they sell the greatest quantity of handmade English saddles of any company in the world, between 30,000 and 50,000 a year. Ronald Reagan, Michael J. Fox, show jumper Aaron Vale, and the Royal Canadian Mounted Police have all ridden in a Stubben. They are made of cow, water buffalo, and elk hides and have a life span of twenty-five to thirty years. Each saddle is marked with a serial number in case of theft, and most riders, including Jackie, have a brass nameplate on the back. The saddle styles, such as "Siegfried," or "Tristan," and others, are named from the operas of Wilhelm Richard Wagner.

OPPOSITE JACKIE TROTS IN PERFECT FORM AT A HORSE SHOW IN VIRGINIA IN THE SUMMER OF 1962.

Jackie often rode in the Siegfried model. "It's the most popular one we've ever built," noted Buddy Baird of Stubben. "This saddle has a very deep seat, and many who hunt prefer it." The cost runs between $750 and $2,500. "Whatever she had she would never compromise, it was always the very best," Wright said. The pre-sale estimate at the Onassis estate sale was $300–500, but Jackie's saddle sold for a staggering $90,500.

During the White House years, Jackie often would shop at Stombock's Fine Riding Apparel, a fixture on M Street in Georgetown for more than one hundred years. C.C. Mills measured the First Lady for breeches several times, taking her waist, hip, inseam, and calf details.

"There would always be three Secret Service men with her," Mills recalled. "One would go to the back, one would be out front, and one would stay in the store. I learned real quick to lock the door when she came in, because people would want to stick their nose in."

"She wasn't modest when I was doing her tailoring," continued Mills. "One day she was only wearing nylon panties, and you just can't do [the measurements] that way. It's a close contact deal." So he asked the First Lady to put on some long underwear.

"On this day, she had two new Secret Service guys and we were in the back a long time in the dressing room, with a slide curtain. We were talking about Middleburg and Paul Fout, and all of a sudden one of the Secret Service guys yanks the curtain."

The First Lady was astounded and scolded him harshly. "I never saw that guy again," Mills said.

The president also ordered jodphur walking shoes from Mills. And when it was somehow decided he would go riding, the riding apparel also came from Stombock's.

President Kennedy's outing on horseback was an event that close friend and then *Newsweek* journalist Ben Bradlee recalled with humor. Bradlee, the revered executive editor of the *Washington Post*, and his wife at the time, Tony, were close friends with the Kennedys. In 1975 Bradlee wrote a book entitled *Conversations With The President*, but he left out the story about the two dashing men mounting up for an afternoon ride through the open fields in Middleburg.

"I'm the worst rider," Bradlee said. "But I was scared he was going to fall off. He wasn't in control and he didn't look like he enjoyed it. It must have offended [Jackie's] sensibilities because it didn't look like he had a good seat to me."

The First Lady continued to retreat to Middleburg as often as possible. Baldrige feared the press would play up the fact she was playing hookey so often. Jackie also scheduled outings with both the Orange County Hunt and the Piedmont Fox Hounds.

The Orange County Hunt was founded in 1900 in upstate New York by a group of industrialists headed by Edward H. Harriman. By 1903 the group

OPPOSITE WHEN THE ORANGE COUNTY HUNT GATHERED AT THE HOME OF AMBASSADOR CHARLES WHITEHOUSE IN NOVEMBER 1962, JACKIE TOOK JOHN FOR A SHORT RIDE.

transferred to the warmer climate of Virginia. Through the years many well-known sporting names have been part of the OCH, including: Oliver Iselin, August Belmont, R. Penn Smith Jr., and Fletcher Harper of the Boston publishing firm.

The territory is approximately twelve by sixteen miles and described in the hunt roster of the weekly *Chronicle of the Horse* as "rolling; moderately wooded; paneled with coops, post and rails, logs on stone walls; and crossed by two main streams from south to north."

Unlike joining a country club or tennis club, one does not apply for membership in any of the 171 hunts in the United States, instead an invitation is extended. Wealth is not a prerequisite. In many parts of the country owning a portion of the land over which the hunt travels is required. Often a genuine affection and deep knowledge of the sport is heavily considered. Initiation dues and fees vary from $1,000 to as much as $50,000. Invited guests pay a capping

fee, usually $25–$100 for a day. The season runs from early fall to early spring, with a winter hiatus during frigid weather. It essentially lasts from harvest to spring planting. A small, engraved fixture card is sent monthly to members with dates and locations of each meeting place, with names such as Old Denton, Glen Welby, and Milestone.

The Orange County Hunt has long maintained an unwritten overnight "toothbrush" rule. The rider must spend the previous night in the territory. When the Prince of Wales visited the area and did not stay overnight, he did not hunt. Throughout the years, the one exception was Jackie, who became an honorary member.

In America, the sport of riding to hounds dates to 1747, when Thomas, Sixth Lord Fairfax, rode over his vast land holdings in Northern Virginia. George Washington was also an enthusiast and wrote of his passion. There was one incident when his hounds ran not far from the capitol. Several congressmen rushed to watch and a few even mounted up and rode off with the hunt.

The early mornings, with dew on the grass and fog hovering across a pond, presented Jackie and her fellow riders a brilliant scene, with more dazzling views from horseback. Today the emphasis is on the sport of watching the hounds work, listening to them in full cry as the distant intricate strains of the hunting horn echo in valleys and resonate through the woods. The long blow to the beat of horses galloping communicates "gone away"—in other words, the hounds have left the covert. When the fox has "gone to ground," riders hear three consecutive rattling blows. The staccato notes are used to excite the hounds and the long notes are used to gather and collect them. At the end of a long day, a desolate, prolonged call, with three high notes and one low drawn out note, signals "going home."

It's all about the chase, and the fox is rarely killed. According to the Master of Fox Hounds Association: "A successful hunt ends when the fox is accounted for by entering a hole in the ground, called an earth. Once there, hounds are rewarded with praise from their huntsman. The fox gets away and is chased another day."

The Secret Service had a nightmare with the First Lady (known by members of the detail as Lace) galloping through the woods and sailing over fences. At first, several men tried to ride, but it was useless trying to keep up with her— an impediment made none the easier by the fact that she resisted the security presence. It was suggested that perhaps someone from the army calvary or the U.S. Equestrian Team might mount up.

The answer finally came in the form of a handsome twenty-seven-year-old U.S. Park Police Private Denis Ayres. "At the time she was the most important woman in the world," he said, thirty years later. "She was such a private person, and the opinion was she didn't want the intrusion."

Ayres, a lifelong horseman, went

straight from rookie school to the mounted division, skipping the walking beat and cruiser patrol. "The Secret Service and the police chiefs got together and decided I would be the detail. My first job was to take Caroline's pony from McLean to Glen-Ora."

Ayres went on to the rank of sergeant major in charge of over ninety horses for the U.S. Park Police in Washington. For more than thirty years, he capitalized on his equestrian abilities, riding with heads of state and many political types, including Commerce Secretary Malcolm Baldrige, Secretary of the Interior William Clark (who rode every day), and President Ronald Reagan. He rode with Lyndon Johnson, of whom he recalled, "He could sit on a horse but he wasn't a horseman. You could kick back with him and have a Jack Daniels." And he rode to hounds with Marilyn Quayle and the Casanova Hunt while her husband Dan was vice president.

With Jackie, he always rode far back in the field with no radio communication.

"It wasn't even a protection detail," he recalled. He also now shudders at the vulnerability of the horses back then, "Anyone could have drugged the horses."

Occasionally Ayres would get a late night telephone call from Jackie wanting to bring someone to ride the next morning. He was able to provide the horses from one of six stables in Washington. There were over thirty miles of bridle paths. "I think it came from cocktail party talk," he said. "They probably started to talk about horses and you could tell it was a self-invite, 'Oh, I love to ride.' " He'd ask, "How well does the guest ride?" And inevitably the guest would have exaggerated his riding skills.

Jackie would bring her guest to Rock Creek Park in Northwest Washington at 10 A.M. "They always came in a station wagon," Ayres said. "When they stepped out, you could tell what kind of day you were going to have. If there wasn't a wrinkle in the boot and they looked like a catalog photo, you were in deep trouble."

Ayres didn't know what kind of day

he was going to have while out with Jackie and the Piedmont Fox Hounds in mid-November 1961.

The oldest hunt in the United States gathered at West View, the white plaster 1830 Federal Southern Delta style home of Kitty and George Robert Slater, not far from the village of Upperville. Master Theo Randolph and other riders in formal attire with top hats and derbies were greeted with a stirrup cup of port. The hounds waited quietly nearby, held in a large circle by huntsman Albert Poe and members of the staff, known as whippers-in.

The field moved south, riding toward the Bunny and Paul Mellon's estate, Little Oak Spring. Photographer Marshall Hawkins was familiar with the territory. Some say he anticipated the route riders would take that morning and drove ahead and waited near a jump. Others recount he was late and just knew where the riders would be jumping. Either way, he waited with his large-format 4-by-5 Speed Graphic in hand. When he pressed the

shutter, he surprised Jackie. Her horse Bit O' Irish skidded and stopped suddenly at a post and rail fence.

The First Lady went flying off over the jump, her proper white-gloved hands outstretched to brace the fall.

"The horse saw Marshall and shut down," Ayres said.

Eve Fout was there too. "Marshall Hawkins jumped in front of the horse and spooked him."

Hawkins, from the small town of Warrenton, Virginia, followed horses all his life. Jackie was not injured, and she remounted, continued, and later even attended a hunt breakfast. The photo of her taking a tumble put Hawkins over the fence, too. His sales soared.

Out of courtesy, Hawkins went to the hunt breakfast to ask permission to use the photo. Jackie politely deferred the question to the president, who was in Washington. She put in a phone call to her husband, begging him to intervene and stop the photo's release. But the president countered, "I'm sorry Jackie,

but when the First Lady falls on her ass, that's news." Hawkins found many buyers for his famous shot, and the photo was wired around the world. *Life* magazine paid Hawkins $3,500 for use, a fee he negotiated from a payphone at a diner in the next town over.

The local weekly paper, *The Fauquier Democrat*, downplayed the event with a five-paragraph item under a small headline: "First Lady Joins Grass Club at Piedmont Hunt Meet." The article correctly stated she'd joined many other extraordinary riders when she was thrown. After all, the horse doesn't know that it's Jackie up there riding.

Nick Arundel, the publisher of the paper, also was out riding that day. The next morning, a Sunday, he received a telephone call from Jackie.

"She said, 'Jack was in a black Irish mood when I fell, and he told me to get rid of the horse.' A black Irish mood, I'll

OPPOSITE JACKIE TOOK A WELL-DOCUMENTED FALL OFF BIT O' IRISH IN NOVEMBER 1961.

143

never forget it," he recalled. "She was sad about it. He was a good hunter but tended to spook."

Arundel bought the horse from her on the phone for a token amount. The horse continued to be a handful and also dumped Arundel off. "He was not only spooky. I was walking him around one day and suddenly I was standing on the ground." He raced the horse in the point-to-point races, occasionally hunted him, and gave him a home for life at his magnificent Merry Oaks Farm.

One little spill wasn't going to stop the determined Jackie. She immediately acquired a new mount. Rufus was a chestnut and white spotted horse on long-term loan from Eve Fout. "This was a horse that we bred," she said. "He carried her well. She got confidence, and when you have a nice horse like this, you ride well. You know it'll go anywhere."

Rufus was bred by accident after the Fouts had turned out a very good jumper mare in the field. Eleven months later, Rufus arrived one morning. He was named for the local vet, Dr. Rufus Humphrey. "You'd have sworn he was a

OPPOSITE JACKIE ON BIT O' IRISH IN THE FALL OF 1962. "SHE ONCE SAID TO ME, 'I'M SO LUCKY TO HAVE A DAY IN THE COUNTRY WITH PEOPLE WHO LIKE THE SAME THING I LIKE,'" SAYS DON YOVANOVICH, A FELLOW FOX HUNTER AND RACEHORSE TRAINER.

Thoroughbred horse, because he was big and had a lot out in front," Eve said. "And we showed him and all kind of stuff."

Rufus was gentle enough for Jackie to walk about with John Jr. in front of the saddle. She rode him on the long trails and took him to several horse shows.

Whether it was by choice or coincidence, Jackie was at a horse show in May 1962, while her husband was off celebrating his forty-fifth birthday at a Madison Square Garden Democratic fundraiser. Mitch Miller, Diana Ross, Louis Armstrong, Ed Sullivan, Ann Margaret, Shirley McLain, and Carol Channing joined the New York City revelry, and Marilyn Monroe sang an infamously whispered version of "Happy Birthday" heard around the world.

Jackie once again sought the refuge of the horse country. She spent the weekend with her horsey friends with whom she felt most comfortable. While the others frolicked in the Big Apple, she rode in the Loudoun Hunt Horse Show. She won a yellow ribbon for third place. And when her friend Paul Fout took a fall from his horse and ended up in the Loudoun County Hospital, she paid him a visit.

The Kennedys' lease on Glen-Ora was about to expire. The rumors were rampant that they would be moving. Jackie longed for a place of her own in the horse country. The *Washington Star* reported, "The most active pre-season sport in Virginia's hunt country this year is debate over frequent reports that President and Mrs. Kennedy are planning to buy an estate in the center of the fox-hunting circuit."

There was talk about thirty-nine acres near the country crossroad called Atoka. The Fouts purchased the land on behalf of the Kennedys from Hubert Phipps for $26,000.

Construction costs were estimated at $50,000. Ben Bradlee made a bet with

PREVIOUS SPREAD FEBRUARY 16, 1963: ON RUFUS AT GLEN-ORA IN MIDDLEBURG.

OPPOSITE JOHN JR. GETS A RIDE WITH HIS MOTHER ON RUFUS IN THE AUTUMN OF 1962.

the president it would cost him more than $100,000. Paul Fout, once again acting as liaison, oversaw construction on the new ranch-style house.

"After three or four months of building, it was no secret," Paul Fout recalled. "Then one day I got a call from the White House; they wanted me to come into Washington to meet with Secretary of Labor [Arthur] Goldberg."

When Fout arrived at the offices, Goldberg scratched his head and said, "We've got a problem." They'd been using non-union workers on the construction site. He was ordered to make changes immediately. "I was getting workers from Fairfax and Winchester." Both places are over an hour away. "Union labor rates were $40 an hour, portal to portal." Ben Bradlee had won his wager, but he never did collect.

On November 10, 1963, the Bradlees and the Kennedys spent a quiet afternoon at the new Middleburg home. Jackie had named it Wexford, after the Irish birthplace of Kennedy ancestors.

(Ronald Reagan later leased this very same place prior to taking office as president.) They all sat outside in the soft air and sipped Bloody Marys.

"I remember watching her ride Sardar," Bradlee said. "Macaroni came up to the house and nuzzled the president as he sat on the ground. It was fairly humorous with his nose as he sniffed all around."

On Monday November 11, 1963 a short Associated Press item was relegated to page B-8 of the *Washington Star:*

President and Mrs. Kennedy spent the third weekend in a row at their new home in the heart of the Virginia horse country, enjoying the ease and seclusion of life away from the White House.

The Kennedys drove to church yesterday morning on a clear, sunny day and joined other parishioners at mass in St. Stephen's the Martyr Roman Catholic Church.

The pastor, the Rev. Albert Pereira, delivered a sermon on the Christian death and had some things to say about the high cost of burials.

"There have been excesses in funerals," *Father Pereira said, "and we ought to heed to the warning concerning the therapy of mourning."*

President Kennedy heard him say at another point that "the saints today are the peacemakers." The chief executive was wearing a black suit with a pinstripe and Mrs. Kennedy a two-piece pink wool suit set off by a black lace scarf and accessories.

The President flew back to Washington by helicopter today to take part in Veterans Day ceremonies at Arlington National Cemetery where he was to lay a wreath on the Tomb of the Unknown Soldier.

Barney Brittle was at Wexford on November 22, 1963, putting last minute touches on a pen and shed for the deer from Ireland. A Secret Service agent approached him and gave him the news that the president had been shot in Dallas.

"That was before it hit the radio," he recalled, "I know something nobody knows. When she left here she told me. Nobody knew they were flying home to Virginia from Dallas and that would have been his first overnight here. He always wanted a boat, his back was so bad and he finally knew he had to give up sailing. They were going to spend more time here. They were walking hand in hand in Dallas, nobody knew. They were going straight to the farm to spend more time together. That's not hearsay; she told me that directly, it didn't come from the servants. So much has been written about their lives up and down and back and forth. And then, that's the sad part. It looked like they were going to get it together."

Lyndon Johnson was sworn in aboard Air Force One on a Bible that Father Pereira had loaned President Kennedy. The Bible somehow disappeared and Father Pereira later received a letter of apology from a member of the Johnson administration.

The next day, navy workers went back to Glen-Ora and filled in the secret communications center under the stable with sand. The direct telephone lines from Paul Fout's office to the White House were severed.

Jackie Kennedy fought through her anguish in shaping every last detail of John Fitzgerald Kennedy's funeral, down to the engraved mass cards and sympathy stationery. She asked for photos, drawings, and records from Abraham Lincoln's funeral. She wanted her husband's service to reflect the same dignity. A phone call was made to the caisson platoon at Fort Myer just across the Potomac River in Virginia. Once again horses would play a significant role.

There were horses throughout the city. When it comes to crowd control, one policeman on a horse equals twelve on foot. There were 220 dignitaries from 102 nations in the cortege. This included West German chancellor Ludwig Erhard, Irish president Eamon de Valera, French president Charles De Gaulle, and Golda Meir, Israel's foreign minister.

Denis Ayres sat on his U.S. Park Police horse, Diablo, on Rhode Island Avenue outside St. Mathew's Church. John Jr. came out and saluted the casket. For the three-mile funeral procession, six gray horses pulled the flag-draped coffin on the same caisson used for the Lincoln funeral. The cacophony of hooves broke the somber stillness. A solitary horse was chosen to follow, symbolizing the slain leader.

C. C. Mills received an urgent phone call at his Georgetown tack shop for boots. He gathered up a used pair from the back room. "A red-headed army sergeant from Fort Myer came to get them and I never saw them again," he said, recalling that he tried to get them back to no avail.

A horse lover watching may have mistaken the lone horse for a Thoroughbred as it pranced up Seventeenth Street. The jet-black horse trotted sideways making his way to Arlington Cemetery. He was a sixteen-year-old quarter horse and Morgan cross, more than sturdy enough to carry the heavy saddle with the boots facing backwards.

The horse became a hero. He appeared in the funerals of presidents Dwight D. Eisenhower, Herbert Hoover, and Lyndon Johnson, and General Douglas MacArthur. Visitors flocked to the stables to visit him. One fan brought him a 180-pound butter pecan cake on his last birthday at the age of twenty-nine. There were 1,500 guests.

Several years after the funeral, Jackie received a letter from the secretary of the Army, asking her if she might want to include him in her stable. She wrote back and politely declined, saying it would be better to have him continue in military service.

His stall remains as a shrine. After twenty-four years of distinguished service, the horse was humanely put down on Februrary 6, 1976. A full military funeral followed. He is buried on the Fort Myer parade ground Summerall Field.

HIS NAME WAS BLACK JACK.

FOLLOWING SPREAD "BLACK JACK" AT PRESIDENT KENNEDY'S FUNERAL.

SOLACE

1964–1994

THE WIDOW KENNEDY WAS NUMB. SHE FELT EMPTY. SHE COULDN'T SLEEP AND COULDN'T EAT.

She confided to friends that she felt her life was over. She moved about tediously. Her loneliness was palpable. It took her eleven days to pack up and move out of the White House. By comparison, Eleanor Roosevelt had moved out almost immediately after the death of her husband, Franklin D. Roosevelt, in 1945.

She didn't know which way to turn. Finally, Averill Harriman, Kennedy's under secretary of state, offered his seven-bedroom Georgetown home to the grieving First Lady after a conversation with John Kenneth Galbraith. The Harrimans temporarily relocated to the Georgetown Inn, and Jackie and her children moved into their red brick house at 3036 N Street, just steps away from the house at number 3307 she once shared with JFK.

When she went shopping in the quaint neighborhood, people gawked. If she felt captive in the White House, these surroundings were overwhelming. She continued to flee to Middleburg for weekends. She rode Sardar during the day, and tried to focus on

PREVIOUS SPREAD AND OPPOSITE JUNE 16, 1967: JACKIE AND HER MOUNT, EMILY, MOVED THROUGH A FIELD NEAR WOODSTOWN HOUSE IN SOUTHERN IRELAND, WHERE SHE AND HER TWO CHILDREN VACATIONED.

Caroline and John. Nights were lonely. Even life in the country was not the same, no matter how hard she tried.

Sometimes she would go for a ride through Rock Creek Park. She pressed on, trying to pull her life together. In December 1963 she bought a fourteen-room house of her own for $175,000. It wasn't long before word was out. Her new address, again a short walk up the street at 3017 N Street, became a stopping point for even more onlookers. "Inquiring photographer" took on a new meaning, as tourists waited on the brick sidewalks with their cameras. A friend described it as a circus.

Jackie continued her forays to the horse country. Her beloved brother-in-law Bobby Kennedy arrived one sparkling morning in a station wagon with his black Lab. As usual, it created a buzz as Jackie and the attorney general came out of the house. She was wearing her riding clothes and he was carrying a wicker picnic basket. It was a splendid spring day for lunch and a ride. The Secret Service was close behind.

Washington just wasn't working, and in 1964 she purchased a fifteen-room apartment in New York City, across the street from Central Park at 1040 Fifth Avenue. It would be home for the next thirty years. She was familiar with the city since childhood. She hired decorator Billy Baldwin and asked him to do the children's rooms much as they'd been in the White House. She wanted them to feel as if they were in familiar surroundings. She ached for some sort of normalcy. Caroline's room had horse pictures and horse books. Now she would be near her sister Lee, who lived at 969 Fifth Avenue, as well as her stepbrother Yusha Auchincloss. Family was everything during this crucial period. But so were her horses.

One of her first phone calls was to Paul Novograd, owner of the Claremont Riding Academy on the upper West Side at 175 West Eighty-ninth Street. Built in

1892 by Edward Bedell, the five-story Romanesque revival building is listed by the New York Landmark Commission as a National Historic Site. Wedged between brownstone houses, it was originally a livery stable. Designed by architect Frank A. Rooke, who specialized in stables and factories, it's made of beige Roman brick, terra cotta, and limestone and is the oldest continuously operated stable in the country. "At first she came and rode with us," Novograd said. All riders need to be screened before going out into the wilds of Manhattan, with honking taxis, incessant sirens, broken fire hydrants, and a ceaseless herd of impatient people. Of course, all the horses have been trained to ignore such distractions.

Jackie no doubt felt she had come home, as barn cats roamed through the creaky wood-paneled office filled with riding helmets, boots, and other bits of tack. The familiar aroma of sweaty horses laced with manure wafted though the air, a product of more than one hundred horses living here, producing fifty-five cubic yards of potential fertilizer. A commercial size elevator or a ramp brings horses to the ground level postage stamp 65- by 75-foot indoor arena for lessons.

Novograd took over from his father, Irwin Novograd, who started as a book-keeper at the stables in 1927 and bought the business in 1943. Over the years, he's dealt with regulars such as Meryl Streep and Jeremy Irons, as well as Robert DeNiro, Christie Brinkley, Matthew Broderick, Andie MacDowell, Sigourney Weaver, Isabella Rosellini, and Richard Dreyfuss. "We know how to respect their privacy," he said.

Once Jackie became acclimated to the horses, she was off and trotting through Central Park. "It doesn't matter who you are—a horse regards you as either a good rider or a bad one," said New York rider and writer Steve Price, who observed Jackie from a distance. "That is, somewhere on the continuum of being a burden."

Novograd arranged to have someone meet her at the Engineer's Gate, north of the Guggenheim Museum at Ninetieth Street and Fifth Avenue. The Claremont rider would have another horse in hand waiting. All she had to do was walk out her front door, cross the street, and go up a few blocks. Jackie, in jodphurs, tweed jacket, and helmet, stepped onto a stone mounting block just inside the gates. The ride took her around the reservoir—now named the Jacqueline Kennedy Onassis Reservoir—to the north meadow and the tennis courts, past the Great Lawn and the Sheep Meadow, with a peek at the Tavern on the Green restaurant, continuing on to the children's playground.

"Most of the time she rode by herself," he recalled. "The other rider followed at a discreet distance to make sure she was okay." The cost was then $25 and is now $65.

She rode several times a week in the mornings. "To ride in the park is a real escape," Novograd said. "With the sweeping vistas, you can't imagine you're in a city. It's like Oz with the greenery. As you trot around the reservoir and you see the skyline rising, it's unreal." The broad five-mile bridle path was part of the 1858 design done by the legendary landscape designer Frederick Law Olmstead.

During this time, Jackie also maintained weekly appointments with a psychiatrist and took up yoga. Horseback riding remained a significant part of her recuperative routine. "Her horse was her counselor, psychologist, and spiritual advisor," Novograd said.

Caroline also went to Claremont for riding lessons. Novograd took her and several others through the park, teaching them to post to the trot, and to keep their heels down and eyes up. "At the time," he said, "she was more interested in cutting up with her friends and gossiping. It was entertainment, not education." For Jackie, it was the best of all worlds.

Jackie began to emerge from her despair. She started to step out at night.

For Easter in April 1966, she took the children to Argentina. They stayed at the San Miguel Ranch in Cordoba. Her itinerary, of course, included an afternoon on horseback. She looked calm and collected as she meandered through the mountains of the region with Dr. Jose A. Martinez de Hoz Jr., president of the Argentine Chamber of Commerce. She wore traditional gaucho attire. Her hands rested on the front of the lamb fleece-lined gaucho saddle. She was relaxed and held the reins on the bridle loosely. She rode a native workhorse called a crillio, known to be sturdy and safe. The tension had lifted.

Two weeks later, she made a trip to Spain without her children. In Madrid, she was mobbed, as everyone wanted to get a peek at the elegant woman. She traveled on to Seville, the glorious center of Andalusia, for the feria, a festival of bullfights and horses.

As the guest of the Duke and Duchess Alba, she rode a majestic white Andalusian. She wore a ruffled shirt, red jacket, leather chaps, and flat top black felt hat—all part of the traditional *traje corto*. The exquisite image of an obviously delighted Jackie appeared on the cover of *Life* magazine.

At the bullfight in the afternoon, she watched as legendary matadors El Cordobes, Paco Camino, and El Viti dedicated the first kill to her. It's a dance of certain death, packed with emotion and feverish energy. Jackie appreciated the sport, the history and the culture . . . but not enough to stay for the predetermined result.

When Jackie rode through the streets in a beautiful horse drawn carriage, she again adapted with the local customs. She pulled her hair up in the *peineta* comb with a long white lace mantilla. That night, she attended the International Red Cross Ball at the Duke of Medinaceli's castle. She was swathed in white mink, a blue Oleg Cassini gown, and glistening diamonds.

Jackie took John-John and Caroline on a six-week summer vacation in Ireland, the land of their father's ancestors, in 1967. They stayed in the sixty-room manor Woodstown House. They visited the village of Dunganstown and saw members of the extended Kennedy clan. They accepted sympathy from residents and relatives. And, they still found time for a beautiful afternoon canter. Jackie rode a horse called Emily and Caroline rode Danny Boy. John's pony, Pal, was very eager to get to the emerald grass. This was one of so many moments the three shared on horseback over the years.

Jackie traveled to Ireland with Peggy and Murray McDonnell and their children, who were great playmates for Caroline and John. McDonnell, a wealthy Wall Street broker, was also a horse lover and a longtime friend. He owned an estate in the horse country of New Jersey.

OPPOSITE WHILE IN SEVILLE APRIL 22, 1966, JACKIE RODE AN ANDALUSIAN WEARING FULL TRADITIONAL ATTIRE.

At first Jackie leased a country place in Long Island and boarded some of her horses out there. She eventually moved her horse operation to New Jersey and bought a six-acre place on Pleasant Valley Road in Peapack for $200,000. It was just over an hour from the city and ten or fifteen minutes away from the McDonnells. She kept her horses at their stables.

The Essex Fox Hounds area is ten by fifteen miles in Somerset County and extends to horse interests in Hunterdon and Morris counties. The towns and villages include Far Hills, Bedminster, Oldwick, Gladstone, and Bernardsville. The land is hilly with miles of white painted fences. Noted architect George Post, who designed the New York Stock Exchange, also designed many of the large homes. Most of the mansions are obscured from view.

Equestrian pursuits are plentiful in the area. The United States Equestrian Team training facility is in Gladstone. George Morris, one of the top show jumping trainers in the U.S., lives in

PREVIOUS SPREAD AND OPPOSITE JACKIE, CAROLINE, AND JOHN ON VACATION IN IRELAND IN 1967.

Pittstown. There are private polo games, steeplechase races, and, of course, fox hunting.

In 1891 fox hunting became a tradition at the Essex Hunt Club, when Charles Pfizer, of pharmaceutical fame and fortune, built two kennels and brought in a pack of hounds. Early members of the organization included James Cox Brady, Stuyvesant Pierrepont, and Richard Whitney. Other influential estate owners included John Jacob Astor, Prudential Insurance founder John Dryden, and American Tobacco Company founder James Buchanan Duke. Some who have come and gone include Malcolm Forbes, King Hassan II of Morocco, John DeLorean, Jacqueline Badger Mars, and money manager Michael F. Price. There are also various members of the Johnson family. "Some are Johnson and Johnson," according to Anthony Knapp, a member of the hunt for thirty-five years, "and some are just Johnson."

The kennels, home to more than ninety brown and white American fox-hounds, are located in Peapack. There, a group of white frame buildings house the hounds (referring to these creatures as "dogs," by the way, would not be proper in this circle) and some horses. The hunts-man, usually a paid staff member, also lives here. He's not to be confused with the master, who is usually a landowner and often wealthy . . . but money is not a requirement for the position.

Annual family subscription fees run from $3,000 to $3,850, depending on how many acres are owned. Initiation fees are equal to the subscription fees and due when notified of election. Individual dues are listed between $1,925 and $2,460 for landowners. Jackie was the first exception to the land owning rule.

Lewis Murdock was master of the hunt when Jackie first moved to the area. "We couldn't go to her and say, 'Sorry old cock, we've got this new rule and you're through,'" he told writer Stephen Birmingham in his 1978 book, *Jacqueline*

Bouvier Kennedy Onassis. "That would
be a pretty crappy thing to do, wouldn't
it? So she stays on. She's never given us
any trouble."

In the field, Jackie was not a New
York celebrity or the former First Lady.
"Nobody bothered her," Knapp said.
She was simply just another horse lover.
Murdock told Birmingham, "Hell, nobody
here is impressed with who she is.
Sometimes I take her and Caroline out
alone. I say, 'Don't ask me any questions;
just watch what I do and do the same
thing.' She never said a damn word, just
did what I showed her. She knows what
she's doing, and she does it damn well.
I never talk to her about anything else.
Having her with us makes no damn
difference to anybody. When we had to
pass the hat for a new truck a while
back, she gave us a hell of a nice check.
She knows half the people in the field by
name, and of course everybody knows
who the hell she is. Hell, maybe she likes
to hunt to get away from the kind of
society life she lives in New York the rest

of the time. But I know she hunts with
us because she likes to hunt—just like
the rest of us. When she's here, she's just
one of us, having a hell of a lot of fun.
Nobody here thinks anything else about
her, one way or the other."

"There was an unwritten rule,"
according to Queenie Kemmerer. "You
gave her her space." Jackie spoke to
everyone and went out of her way to learn
everyone's name. "When she said 'Hello
Queenie,' she made you feel at ease."
In one freak moment, Caroline's horse
pulled the bridle off her husband
Doug Kemmerer's horse, leaving him
with no ability to control his mount.
If the horse had decided to run away,
Kemmerer would have had quite a
challenge to stop him. Jackie quickly
jumped off her horse and helped put the
bridle back on.

When the United States Equestrian
Team was having a charity gala, she gladly
lent her name as honorary chairman.
But she did not attend. "She always went
to the hunt breakfast, but never to the

hunt ball," Queenie said. "And she always had a stirrup cup." (A traditional sip of brandy offered to riders before setting off for the hunt.)

Joan Scher rode out of her White Oak Farm in Far Hills with Jackie for twenty-five years. Joan rode side-saddle. "She was always very interested in it," Joan said. Frequently the conversation turned to their children. "My son was getting married about the same time as Caroline and she asked me, 'How many coffee cups does Greg have? Because Caroline only has three.'"

Jacque Dreyer was out on her new horse Root Road one day. "I'd put a red ribbon in his tail," she recalled. (The red ribbon is to warn others your horse might kick.) "Jackie didn't see it; she was used to seeing me on my big, wide, part Percheron–part Thoroughbred. Everyone could ride into her to stop." (Some riders, out of desperation to slow down or stop, will often bump into the back of the horse in front.)

Jacque Dreyer's horse struck out. "He was a former racehorse and didn't want anyone near him, much less threaten to pass. And I thought, this is how I'm going to get in the papers. But she [Jackie] apologized profusely." Jackie and her horse were unhurt.

"Nobody paid any attention to her," Dreyer continued. "Everyone was involved in their own stuff." When riding at a gallop all attention must be paid to making potential split second decisions: left, right, hold tight, give the horse his head. And when the horses pause or rest between runs, idle chitchat, known as "coffee housing" is also frowned upon.

The Kennedy children also were treated just like all the others. When Bill Dreyer was working as ringmaster at a horse show, he caught a bunch of kids sitting on a fence. "He told them all to get down off," his wife Jacque Dreyer

OPPOSITE AFTER SPENDING MAY 27, 1966, IN SECLUSION IN OBSERVANCE OF THE LATE
PRESIDENT'S FORTY-NINETH BIRTHDAY, JACKIE AND CAROLINE RODE IN THE SAINT
JOSEPH'S CHURCH HORSE SHOW AND CHILDREN'S FAIR IN MOUNT VERNON,
NEW JERSEY, AND FINISHED IN SECOND PLACE IN THE FAMILY CLASS.

recalled. "Caroline didn't get off and he looked at her and said, 'You, too, Caroline.' And Jackie looked over and smiled as if to say 'thank you.'"

Jackie and Caroline both competed in several small New Jersey horse shows, such as the St. Bernard's School Horse Show in Gladstone. They stood in line at the hamburger stand along with all the other participants. Jackie filled out the entry forms just as her mother had done for her. Jackie now rode in the family class with Caroline, just as her mother had once done with her. And, each time, they brought home numerous ribbons. They competed at the Saint Joseph's Church Horse Show and Children's Fair in May 1966, after spending the previous day in seclusion honoring JFK's birthday. They took second place and never received any preferential treatment from the judges. John Jr. also joined in the horse activities. The three Kennedys were regular competitors at the annual Essex Hunter Trials each fall.

When Jackie married Aristotle Onassis in October 1968, there were two hundred armed security men, patrol

OPPOSITE CAROLINE JUMPS OVER A SPLIT RAIL FENCE IN THE COUNTRYSIDE OF NEW JERSEY WHILE OUT WITH THE ESSEX FOX HOUNDS IN THE EARLY SEVENTIES.

boats, and helicopters stationed on his Greek island of Skorpios for the wedding. She confessed to Oleg Cassini that she on longer wanted to dwell on the painful past. She wanted to move into a new life. And that new life happened to come with many new luxuries and indulgences. While she once traveled on the private Kennedy plane called the Caroline, she now had the entire Olympic Airways fleet at her fingertips. The Kennedy family yachts Honey Fitz and Marlin must have seemed like something that would float in the swimming pool once Jackie stepped aboard the sleek Christina. A converted Canadian frigate, it was longer than a football field, with a crew of fifty, two chefs, and forty-two telephones.

Onassis recognized her love of horses. He created a stable with Arabian horses and Shetland ponies on Skorpios. It was not to her liking, for although she would frequently ride a different style while on a brief visit to a foreign country, she preferred the traditional English style of riding. One part of her life would not change. Just one month after the marriage, she was back on her horses in New Jersey.

November 22, 1968, marked the fifth anniversary of the president's death. Jackie spent the day in seclusion. However, the very next day, she began a tradition on horseback with Caroline and John that would last for many years. Onassis was there but did not ride.

In fox hunting, the custom of riding on Thanksgiving weekend is revered. Children come home from boarding school and college, and all the equestrian members of the family gather. The Essex Fox Hounds would meet at Ellistant, owned by Hank Slack.

Jackie needed to borrow horses or ponies for Caroline and John from neighbors and friends. Hers were not suitable. Michele McEvoy Grubb, a

PREVIOUS SPREAD JACKIE, JOHN, AND CAROLINE RIDING OUT WITH THE ESSEX FOX HOUNDS IN BEDMINSTER, NEW JERSEY, IN THE EARLY SEVENTIES.

OPPOSITE NOVEMBER 22, 1979: JACKIE AT THE PATERNITI FARM DURING THE ESSEX HUNT CLUB'S ANNUAL THANKSGIVING DAY FOX HUNT HELD IN BEDMINSTER, NEW JERSEY.

champion horsewoman and neighbor, recalls how Jackie asked about her children by name when she called to borrow a pony. She then sent a beautiful thank-you note on her signature Bar Harbor blue stationary.

"With their helmets on, people couldn't tell one kid from another," Anthony Knapp said. He described both children "as game as could be" and added, "After riding hard all day like that, they probably couldn't get out of bed the next day."

The local newspapers were quickly alerted to Jackie's annual outing. Headlines in the the *Newark Star Ledger* declared: "Jackie Proves Her Skill on Horseback, Holiday Fox Hunt a Kennedy Tradition" and "Tally ho for Jackie in Jersey." Her relationship with equine photographers was contrary to her much publicized battle with the paparazzi. "It's not true that she hated being photographed," one friend noted. "She loved being photographed on her horses or while jumping a fence." She used the pictures as a learning tool, to improve her form. She gave her grooms David Lloyd, Boonie Smith, David Corum, and Jimmie Mason

OPPOSITE JACKIE ADJUSTS JOHN JR.'S STIRRUPS BEFORE GOING OUT WITH THE ESSEX FOX HOUNDS IN BEDMINSTER, NEW JERSEY.

gifts of the photos and would even hand them a camera to take more pictures.

Photographer Richard Corriden took many photos of Jackie while she was riding in New Jersey. "I took images as she was warming up at the hunter pace," he said. "I told her I had them, and she looked at them and liked them, and gave me her address."

In Virginia, she was very cooperative with photographers who wanted to shoot her on horseback. Most of these photographers were either friends or professionals who specialized in taking pictures of horses. "As reclusive as she was, she was always tremendously friendly and open to having her picture taken," said Malcolm Matheson III, a member of the Orange County Hunt. "I always took a lot of pictures and she liked me and we got along."

"I didn't specifically seek her out, but when the opportunity was around I got her along with everyone else," said photographer Raymond Utz, also a blacksmith and avid fox hunter.

Jackie instinctively knew which photographers were part of the regular group following the horses. A professional photographer from the city or a new agency would stand out in the country simply by his wrong clothing alone. One day an unknown photographer showed up and asked her permission to take a picture. "She told him, 'I guess one will be okay,'" Utz said. "But he kept on shooting, and she turned to go back to the barn and asked me to come with her. She wanted to have her picture taken with her groom Jimmie Mason."

"She wasn't bothered at all," according to Douglas Lees, who snapped several portraits while she discussed strategy before an event one morning. His photo of her jumping a stone wall later that afternoon shows Jackie in near perfect form. Her secretary, Nancy Tuckerman, called to order several copies. "I'm gun shy," he added, referring to the camera's shutter and the previous incident, when all the blame went to the photographer and Jackie fell. "I don't like to take pictures of people falling." He uses a 300mm lens. "I try to get as far away as possible. This is an amateur sport and I don't want to cause a problem."

While still in the White House, Jackie had press secretary Pam Turnure send photographer Howard Allen a letter. Allen remained one of her favorite photographers. "As you know, you are the only person who has taken special pictures, at her request, of her and the children in the country," Turnure wrote on March 8, 1963, "and you are and will continue to be the only person authorized to release these riding pictures when she feels it is the right time."

Jackie's annoyance had been piqued by Marshall Hawkins' photo of her falling off her horse, not to mention the subsequent wide release of the photo, and she was generally known for having a long memory. However, twenty-seven years later, that grudge had apparently been forgotten as she wrote the foreword to a collection of his work. *A Field of Horses,* published in 1988 and written by James

L. Young, even included the famous falling-off photo. "In all my discussions with her, she never even alluded to the photo," Young said. And when he was stymied about which photos to include and which to edit out, Jackie came to the rescue. "She came over one afternoon after fox hunting and laid all the pictures out on the floor. She pushed the pictures around. She was in riding clothes, crawling on the floor. She had quite an eye and an instinctive appreciation for what would look good."

In 1975 Jackie became the widow Onassis. She began a fresh career in publishing the following year. She took a job at Viking Press as a consulting editor for $200 a week.

In 1977 she settled with the Onassis estate for a reported $20 million and resigned from her job at Viking. After some passage of time, she became an acquiring editor at Doubleday. On the weekends, she fled the fast and furious city life for the tranquil atmosphere with her horses. She met horseman Scott

Milne later that year. Now in his late forties, he was then in college and exercising field hunters. When the job of taking care of Jackie and her horses became available, Milne recalled, "I stepped right in."

He worked for her in New Jersey for seventeen years training the horses, taking them to horse shows, and attending to every detail. "We would borrow the horses from the McDonnells or other neighbors when Caroline or John Jr. would come to ride. Each time I would ask myself, 'Where am I going to find something to tote these kids around?'"

He said, "Caroline has a fantastic feel and a great eye. If she set herself to it she would be a fantastic rider. And John was just athletic and could do anything. But can you imagine not riding all year and then going out there for three hours?"

"John didn't ride that much," said Peggy Murray, who worked at Bevel Saddlery and also helped Scott with the horses. "He did it for his mother. We would suit him up in clothes and she just loved it. It was great. Other than Thanksgiving, it was just a trail ride. He preferred bikes."

Peggy recalled the day John just turned up unannounced at the barn. "I turned around and he said, 'Hey Peggy.' And I said, 'John Kennedy, you scared the hell out of me.' He wasn't that crazy about the horses. He just pedaled the bike and came in the barn and he acted so interested. He asked, 'What horse is this?' or 'Is this my mother's horse or the one for sale for a lot of money?'"

In addition to Jackie's horses, Scott had several of his own in training. One was a show horse named Over Abundance. The horse was having a very successful season, winning blue ribbons all along the way. He was for sale for a large sum of money. "In those days, six figures was a lot of money," Murray said. "Nowadays it wouldn't get you a three-foot horse. She was beside herself. She was so impressed

with the horse, not the fact he was worth the money. She was impressed that Scott had done all this work with the horse by himself. And now the horse was going to Madison Square Garden."

For the National Horse Show in New York City, exhibitors and trainers have to get up in the middle of the night in order to work the horses in the unfamiliar indoor surroundings. Practice hours begin at three in the morning and last until eight and Jackie wanted to see the action. "She wanted to see the horse go. But mind you, only hardcore horse people in boots are there at that hour. She was on her way to work at Doubleday. There are only a few people in the seats. And we look up and there she is waving to us," Peggy recalled.

Like many, Scott found the setting and the horses intoxicating. He eventually quit college and went to work on perfecting Jackie's technique in the hunting field. "She had this dashboard seat with her feet out in front. She was a total passenger," he said, meaning her form on the

horse put her in a passive position and she needed to become more assertive.

She rode as frequently as possible to improve her technique and style. "She worked as hard as anyone could. She was here on Friday, Saturday, and Sunday, and sometimes more often." She and Scott went hunting together. "There are ditches and branches and you just can't run up to the jump and yee haw. How about the hole on the other side? It offers a new sense of appreciation for horses. Your horse is your best friend. He saves your life. After three or four hours they're all tucked up. When galloping, it's the epitome of what we all feel with the breeze."

Scott had the horses groomed impeccably. The standards of grooming for hunting are not as intense as for showing. He'd braid their manes and have them covered in plaid blankets as they stepped off the horse van at the meet. "She said to me one day, 'You people like to dress

OPPOSITE PAMELA HARRIMAN AND JACKIE SHARED A LOVE OF HORSES. HERE AT THE PIEDMONT HUNT AT LITTLE OAK SPRING, THE ESTATE OF PAUL MELLON, IN THE AUTUMN OF 1983.

the horses up like Barbie dolls with the blankets and bandages all in green,'" Peggy Murray said.

"I was very respectful and said, 'I don't agree. Now Mrs. Onassis, when we go to the hunt, I want you to look around at some of the horses and isn't it nice your horse is presented properly?' Scott and I really had it played up a bit, almost like show horses."

Jackie appreciated the work put into turning out the horses perfectly groomed. "She respected people who didn't yes her to death. She said, 'Peggy, you always speak your mind.'"

When fox hunting, Peggy recalled, "She loved to gallop and go fast."

"The men thought they could impress her jumping a big jump," Scott said. "No way. She was right up there. It was funny to watch them."

Sheila Wolk, a member of the Old Dominion Hunt near Hume, Virginia, remembered when Jackie came out as a guest one day. "The lady could ride. She rode strong in front of the men, over tough stone walls in rough country. It was March and cold and she never pulled up."

Jackie and Meg Gardner, master of the Middleburg Hunt, once were separated from the other riders. "She never panicked," Meg recalled. "She said, 'Oh Meg, I know the countryside so well, I know we'll find them.' Well, we rummaged around for an hour and finally caught up."

One of her horses was a large bay called Town Clown, nicknamed Toby. Scott didn't think he was entirely appropriate. "You'd canter to the jump and he'd look for something to spook at. If something caught his eye in the hedgerow at the last minute, it would be like he was saying, 'Oh jump, yeah,' and then he'd go off."

Scott tried different bits on the bridle, some stronger and perhaps more effective. In his opinion, it wasn't working. Many horses, after so many years in the hunting field, become overly eager. The horses hear the hounds and anticipate the next act will be a long run. "He would fold his legs well, but he dragged her to the jump."

With her permission, he went in search of a new horse. "She learned she had to have several horses," Scott said. He connected with Irishman Eamon Hughes, a New Jersey based horse trainer. "His barn is an oasis in the middle of a large development of homes," Scott recalled of the first day he spotted Be Frank.

The large gray gelding was a seven-eighths Irish bred: part Thoroughbred and part something else. "Frank was the best of everything," Scott said. "Handsome and with more bone than a Thoroughbred, but not heavy like a Warmblood. He cantered correctly. And he was the best in the air. The horse loped over a four and a half foot oxer.

"Finding him was a miracle. Supposedly, in Ireland, he did show jumpers. He came off the corner and would backpedal until you could see your way and feel to the jump. He sits back, you couldn't miss the distance if you tried."

After weeks of searching for the perfect horse, Scott was ecstatic. He put in a call to New York. "I called the secretary, Lee Nasso, and said, 'We have to buy this horse.' And she tells me, 'Scott, she's gone for a month. We have to wait.'"

Beside himself, Scott begged and the sellers continued to wait. The price of the horse was about $15,000, fairly steep for a field hunter. "He was so scopey. You felt you could handle any jump. I almost felt he could have been a working hunter in the show ring."

Jackie planted a small apple orchard on her place and moved her own horses to another stable. She had three horses: Toby, Frank, and Midnight. She rented a barn on the back of a tract of land owned by the Edgecomb family. She called her stable Red Gate. "It was very isolated," Scott said. "There were no people, just animals, her horses, the

squirrels." The barn had a center aisle with stalls on each side. It was made of wood, which was stained to a faded brown color. Some of the stalls opened to large pastures. "It wasn't fancy, but it was clean and neat and workmanlike. It wasn't like the Mellons with the polished brass." There was a tack room, a wash stall, and a riding ring, which they seldom used. Scott lived in an apartment off the back of the barn.

In the early fall, Jackie enjoyed slow, quiet walks while getting the horses prepared for the hunt season. "She loved to just roam around, just the two of us. We'd be walking past a place and she would spot an orchard and say, 'Come on, let's walk up here.' We'd go up the driveway, and we'd pick a few apples and bring them back to the barn."

Back in the stables, Be Frank had a trick.

"If you stood in front of the stall with a treat and said, 'Give me a kiss,' he'd curl his upper lip and kiss you. He would never bite. He was a handsome,

talented horse, but as a pet he'd slime all over your cheek." And he slimed all over Jackie's cheeks many times. She always arrived with carrots and apples. And she always pitched in to help with grooming or tacking up the horses.

Jackie loved to compete in the horse events. Each autumn the various hunts produce a hunter pace or field hunter trials. It serves as a fund-raiser for the hunt and provides a way for riders to measure their ability. Scott would go out with Jackie the day before the event and walk the course. They'd plot the route and look at the jumps closely. "She was thrilled," he said.

"I was fascinated to see her ride. When she rode I was favorably impressed," recalled Cora Cushny, one of the judges at the Essex Hunter Trials and the roommate of Jackie's sister Lee at Miss Porter's. "She had a nice horse and it was a good combination. And I thought, 'This is good.'" Jackie won the Lady Ardmore

Challenge Trophy three times and retired the trophy.

Jackie rode with Scott in the Essex Hunter Pace Event, a cross-country type of race. Scott rode one of Jackie's other horses, a big black she called Midnight. A former steeplechase horse and a Thoroughbred, his registered name was Mail List. His reputation was that he liked to run fast in the beginning of the race. He was finished by the first quarter mile.

The third member of the hunter pace group was Jeanne Hamilton Troast, a member of Essex for thirty years. "I knew Jackie to say hello, as many of us did," Troast said. "She loved my big, dark, bay, flashy horse. We talked and she was on Town Clown and the two horses were pinging off each other. She liked it if you were a goer and didn't take life too seriously. It was where she could play."

As the three were racing, they came upon a new coop on a rise. "And I'm thinking, 'Oh my, it's big.'" They paused. "And, I said, 'Let's ask Scott,' and before I knew it, she whipped Frank around and she was over the fence." The others had no choice but to follow. "We just missed winning. The next year we went back and we were second or third." Jackie later sent a note thanking Jeanne for joining the event. Many of her horsey friends cherish the notes on her Bar Harbor blue stationery. When she wrote from home, they were simply engraved 1040 Fifth Avenue. When they were written while traveling, her stationery had the scallop shell of a pilgrim at the top.

The horses remained in Scott's care for nine months of the year. For the other three, Jackie traveled back to Virginia, to the area of Middleburg that had always been so precious to her. The horses stayed at Paul Mellon's estate and she kept a cottage close by.

PREVIOUS SPREAD JACKIE AND BE FRANK AT THE ORANGE COUNTY HUNT TEAM EVENT AT OLD WHITEWOOD, THE PLAINS, VIRGINIA.

OPPOSITE NOVEMBER 5, 1989: JIMMIE MASON, JACKIE ON BE FRANK, AND LEROY MOORE AT THE VIRGINIA FIELD HUNTER CHAMPIONSHIPS AT OAKENDALE, MIDDLEBURG.

In March 1981 she rode in the Piedmont Pairs Race at Salem Farm, near Upperville, with James Young, known as Jimmy, one of the joint masters of the Orange County Hunt. Jackie was entered to compete with another rider from New Jersey. At the last minute, the other horse was lame and Jimmy stepped in on his former steeplechase horse, Zeke.

While deliberating on tactics, he asked if she wanted to try for the ideal time or go as fast as possible. The three-mile course took them over twenty-five jumps. She told him to use his best judgment and she'd follow. They galloped over stone walls, logs, and split rail fences. They finished the course two minutes faster than anyone else, which did not necessarily ensure a win. Each time Jimmy looked back to check on Jackie, she indicated she was okay.

OPPOSITE OCTOBER 29, 1989: JACKIE AND BE FRANK AT THE END OF THE DAY OF COMPETITION AT THE ORANGE COUNTY HUNT TEAM EVENT, THE PLAINS, VIRGINIA. "ALL SHE WANTED WAS TO BE IN THE COUNTRY," BARNEY BRITTLE SAID. "ALL SHE WANTED WAS FOR PEOPLE TO LEAVE HER ALONE."

Jimmy felt his horse was out of control and knew the judges would discount this. They had no chance for a prize but patiently waited with the others. They stood in the brisk air as the results were announced. Jackie told him that she thought they deserved at least a mention. "This was my first inkling of Jackie's competitiveness," he later said. "I was to learn that winning wasn't always significant to her but competing with some distinction was."

"Although she knew it didn't really matter," another rider said, "she was very competitive and was perfectly happy to win."

Horsewoman Barbara Graham was one of Jackie's closest hunting pals in Virginia. Jackie took her picture back in 1952 when she had been the Inquiring Photographer. "We lost touch for a while and then when she started to come down here to hunt, we got together," Barbara said. "She never talked about the past at all. She left it all behind. She never talked about Ethel or the Kennedys.

She never mentioned Onassis. It was all just out of her life. I was glad I knew her."

They hunted side by side in the mornings and then drove around the countryside in the afternoon to explore various interests. "We connected because she was so down to earth. We just had fun and did fun things." They traveled the country lanes in Barbara's vintage Subaru station wagon, nicknamed Myrtle.

Jackie loved to search for antiques. They visited the Delaplane Country Store one afternoon. Located along a railroad track at an obscure crossroad, it's known mostly by locals as a cherished source of well-priced, well-chosen antiques. One day, they ran into actor Robert Duvall, also a member of the Middleburg community.

"When we got back in the car, she said to me, 'Barbara, can you imagine, I met Robert Duvall at the Delaplane Store?'"

OPPOSITE MARCH 1981: JACKIE AND JIMMY YOUNG DISCUSS STRATEGY FOR THE PIEDMONT PAIR RACE IN MIDDLEBURG.

Piedmont Fox Hounds

40th ANNUAL

Point-To-Point Races

Hunter Pair Race
Old Fashioned Point-To-Point

Sat., March 28, 1981

Salem Course opposite
Upperville Horse Show Grounds
near Upperville, Va.

Price: One Dollar

---

4 — 6—5

HUNTER PAIR RACE

6:30 opt. time   10:30 A.M.   7:01

Optimum time. Over natural country flagged course. Rider &
owner member of recognized hunt, horse to have been regularly
and fairly hunted. Catch weights.

OWNER	RIDER
Pair 1	
Loudoun Hunt	
Karen Clarke	Owner
RED COAT	
ch. g., a.	
Jan Jocich	Owner
BIT O'HONEY	
buckskin m., 6.	
Pair 2	
Warrenton Hunt	
Feroline Burrage	Owner
WINKS	
br. g.	
Orange County Hunt	
Charles S. Whitehouse	Owner
DAGANELLI	
br. g.	
Pair 3	
Essex Hunt	
Jacqueline Onassis	Owner
TOWN CLOWN	
b. g., a.	
Jacqueline Onassis	Frank Richardson
CHEROKEE CREEK	
b. g., a.	
Pair 4	
Piedmont Fox Hounds	
Mrs. T.A. Randolph	T.L. Higginson, Jr.
PUDDLE DUCK	
ch. m.	
Mrs. T.A. Randolph	Michael Elmore
MR. CHIPS	
gr. g., a.	

(5)

OPPOSITE JACKIE DEMONSTRATES EXCELLENT FORM WHILE
MAINTAINING FOCUS.

" 'Well,' I said, 'he's probably driving back home saying, "I can't believe I met Jackie Onassis at the Delaplane Store." ' "

Jackie wanted to visit the Piedmont Fox Hound kennels. "She asked me, 'What do the puppies do? What do they eat?'" Each outing was different. One day they had a flat tire. It was cold and getting dark quickly. A farmhand came to their rescue but really couldn't help much. The two women changed the tire. "This is what you call coming down to earth," Graham recalled. "We knew more than the guy who came off the farm to help change it."

Barbara is a successful race horse trainer. She broke Kentucky Derby and Preakness winner Spectacular Bid. Her own horse, Vodka Talking, was a stakes winner. "Jackie loved one of my race horses and she would call and ask, 'When is Princess Pickle going to run again?' "

Training racehorses at her 400-acre Still Meadow Farm is a middle-of-the-night/early-morning career. Barbara's workday is over at noon. "Sometimes when I'd drive up to my house, she'd be waiting for me at the back door with sandwiches from the Upper Crust." Jackie adored the local bakery and had a sweet tooth for their "cow puddle" cookies, loaded with pecans and brown sugar.

She felt comfortable with her horsey friends. "She could prop her feet up and lay back," Graham said. "One night she tried to show several of us what yoga was. We didn't know. She got down on the den floor and tried to teach us. We laughed for an hour over it all."

Jackie liked to watch Barbara break yearlings to the saddle. "When I was building a shed for the horses, she said, 'You could put bedrooms out there and that's where I'll camp out.' She was really very lonesome." She also wanted to educate herself about the conformation of the horses and would frequently go to the fields with Barbara to look at the foals.

"She loved to take photos of old houses," Barbara continued. "We drove around one day with architect Tommy Beach." In addition to adding a wing on Bunny Mellon's expansive private horticulture library, Beach designed the Sporting Library and several distinctive houses in Middleburg. He describes his style as, "a refined Virginia farmhouse with a flare for the Federal design."

When Barbara renovated the back of her 1780 stone farmhouse, Jackie made suggestions. "I had one of the windows propped open with a stick. She went with me to Leesburg to pick out the new windows." For the expansion of the porch, Jackie walked around the back of the house. She studied the lines of the roof and the angle of the side of the house for a few minutes and came up with the concept of incorporating a stone retaining wall as part of the remodeling. "It was perfect," Barbara said, showing off the results.

The cottage where Jackie stayed was a former chicken house that she had refurbished. "At one time, there were chickens upstairs. She loved the high porch and had a rocker out there. I don't think she had a dress in the closet down here." At the end of the day, Jackie would sit outside and have a glass of wine and a cigarette.

Barbara and Jackie would often go to dinner at the home of Gail and Jim Wofford. Gail had been a master of Piedmont, and Jim is a former Olympic medalist and one of the top coaches in the equestrian discipline of three-day eventing. Sometimes they'd eat at the Coach Stop, a favorite with the locals. "The people who lived in Middleburg didn't bother her. She loved it here, but she knew the boyfriend [Maurice Tempelsman] was there in New York, and her family."

"The assumption was she always had dinner plans," said horse trainer Don Yovanovich, who struck up a friendship

JACKIE ON BE FRANK WITH FELLOW EQUESTRIAN EDIE SMART
ON LADY'S FAVORITE IN THE BACKGROUND.

with Jackie in the hunt field. "She usually went home to a bath and a book."

One day while riding back home, Don invited Jackie to dinner at the Red Fox Inn with his wife, Robyn, and several others. He reserved a small room, and they all entered from the back door. "She was far more approachable than people will ever know. She was generous with her time. She never rushed off when people would talk to her at the Coach Stop," he said. "She always let people talk their fill."

"We developed a rapport," Don said. "When she saw I won a race, she wrote me a note: 'How nice to have another win.'"

One time, Jackie asked Don if he had anyone else in his barn who hunted. "I said yes, there's a girl who is too shy to speak to you and if you get a chance to, say hello to her. She asked her name and told me to tell her to jog up to her. Before Michelle could say a word, she said, 'Michelle, how are you?' They talked for ten minutes as we finished the day. They chatted on, and it's something Michelle will never forget until the day she dies."

Jackie was relentlessly inquisitive, and always wanted to know more about the animals she so loved. "I always rode [former] steeplechase horses and she admired their way of going," Don said. "She wanted to know how to make her horses go better. We would talk about different bits [to use on the bridle]. But it was up to her to make the changes."

Jackie took many riding lessons. "For all her grandeur, she was just like a regular customer," remembered trainer Snowden Clarke. "She didn't expect anything above and beyond. She called me from the local hair house, her headquarters, and you could hear the hair dryers."

She wanted to work on going over a drop jump, where the ground is lower on the far side of the jump and the horse does not see it until he takes off. "She told me she needed help getting with her horse. It was never his fault. I was most impressed from the first time she called. It was never the horse's fault. It was what *she* could do to make it a better horse. Some of the times, riders put more of the focus on the horse."

Snowden worked with Jackie. "I told her to keep her eyes up. You can't be too foreword on the horse's neck. That was one time. We just talked about it. And then we were hunting and there was a drop jump and she jumped it. She looked over at me giving me a knowing glance, acknowledging she'd kept her eyes up as we had worked on. She never said anything, just a knowing look."

There were other lessons jumping over fences in his ring at Rock Ridge Farm. She always scheduled the lessons herself. "And one day it was raining and we didn't cut it short at all." Another friend recalls a rainy day out hunting in a downpour. "Don't you think we should go in?" the friend begged. To which Jackie replied, "Oh, not yet, we're already wet and, who knows, something wonderful might happen."

"She rode great," said Clarke, a third generation Virginia horseman. "She was good. I wasn't teaching her anything she didn't know. I was reminding her and fine-tuning her skills. It was a critique each time, not a lesson."

Grand Prix Show Jumper Ian Silitch gave Jackie lessons almost every week for two years during the late eighties. "I was nervous at first. And my girlfriend at the time went wild. But [Jackie] was so normal and all she wanted to do was ride horses."

Silitch has won over forty-five Grand Prix events in the show ring. He, too, worked on reminding Jackie to keep her eyes up. "I told her you have to believe your horse is going to go over the jump. If he didn't get off the ground, then get a new one. It is very simple. Life is too short to dance with an ugly woman and certainly too short to ride a horse that doesn't go."

She found that every day out riding was a challenge. "I think it was for this reason that she found fox hunting so exciting. You could never tell what might happen next," Ambassador Charles Whitehouse recalled in May 1994. He first met Jackie in the summer of 1946. "It was right after the war and my parents and her parents were friends. I rode with her up in Newport and down here. She was an enchanting young lady and I dated her before she married Jack. She also was very brave and loved flirting with the dangers of the chase. 'That wall seemed awfully big,' she would say with a smile, having soared over it on one of her lovely horses. She also took the inevitable crashes and falls with equanimity—in a way they validated the danger that added spice to the day."

In March 1992 Jackie fell while out hunting with Piedmont. This time she was rushed to the Fauquier Hospital in Warrenton, after the rescue squad waded across a creek to get to her. Trainer Snowden Clarke was there. "We were near the Plaskitts at Bear's Den," he said. Both Jackie and the horse went down. "It was a misjudgment on both their

OPPOSITE NOVEMBER 9, 1990: JACKIE AND BE FRANK SAIL OVER A CHICKEN COOP.

parts. I helped the medic across the stream on the back of my horse."

"If you do this game or anything like it, then you know you're going to have accidents," Barbara Graham commented. "She was a top rider; it just happens. Any type of horses, showing, I don't care who you are."

She was often in Middleburg during the anniversaries of JFK's death. On one dreary November day during the early 1980s, she wandered through the shops in the village alone. She bought a few Christmas ornaments at the High Horse Antiques shop. When the shopkeeper filled out the Visa card information, she realized the significance of the date. She took Jackie's hand as she leaned over the glass top showcase to sign.

"I'm so very sorry," she said.

To which Jackie replied, "Thank you, I just wanted to be alone today."

On November 20, 1993, Jackie was out hunting in Virginia when she was thrown and knocked unconscious for a short time. Dave Simpson, Middleburg's chief of police, reported, "She gave us quite a scare." A member of the rescue squad said she was in shock. She spent the night at the Loudoun Hospital Center.

Some have speculated this was the beginning of the end for Jackie, and while in the hospital the doctors discovered cancer. "Last year [1993] I rode with her for the tenth time in the Orange County Pairs," Ambassador Whitehouse recalled. They finished in second place. "I told her I get out of breath. She told me, 'I can hardly do it all,' but I didn't believe that—she jogged out all around the park every day.

"I asked her, 'Did you get a checkup? How did you find out about this?' Because right now so many people are saying she knew about it for much longer. But that's nonsense. She told me she had the flu and had some funny bumps and went to the doctor and that's how she found out."

After suffering from stomach pains and a constant cough, and noticing some

OPPOSITE JACKIE RECEIVES THE WILLIAM CHADWELL MEMORIAL TROPHY FROM HUNTSMAN ROD CHADWELL AT THE FIFTY-SECOND ESSEX FOX HOUNDS HUNTER TRIALS, OCTOBER 4, 1992, IN PEAPACK, NEW JERSEY.

swollen lymph nodes, Jackie went for tests. Her ailment was diagnosed as non-Hodgkin's lymphoma.

Her friend Barbara Graham recalled, "The last time she called was three weeks before she died. She said, 'I will see you in the fall.' I said, 'That's right. Can't wait.' I know she was thinking of riding. And that was the last time we spoke. I knew it was her way of saying goodbye."

Scott Milne last saw Jackie at Easter before she died. She came to ride her horses. "We'd had a horrible winter and spring was forever coming." She brought her granddaughters, Rose and Tatiana. They, too, carry on the equestrian tradition, taking lessons on Long Island and visiting Middleburg for beagle hunting.

Jackie took them to hunt eggs and bought them rabbits, just as she had done for Caroline. "She felt she didn't want them to shrink back when a neighbor's dog came around. She didn't want them to say, 'Oh no, a dog, mommy,' and then hide behind someone. Caroline just had

Jack and they all came to the stable." Her constant companion, Maurice Tempelsman, was there too, taking a walk.

Jackie rode twice that weekend. "She was wearing a wig and when she tried to put the hard hat on it was tight. She wasn't afraid to admit she was wearing it and asked me to help her." They went on their last ride together, walking and trotting and talking. "The real Jackie was her horse life," he said, "it brought her tremendous joy."

"I never believed she wasn't going to get well, and I called up one day and said, 'I'd appreciate it if I didn't hear health bulletins on the media; could you call me?' We were like family. Once she was gone, John and Caroline didn't get it. You existed, but just as an employee. I didn't want to add to Caroline's pain, but I cried until there were was no more moisture."

"When I heard she was ill, I automatically sent her a note. 'You're going

OPPOSITE IN OCTOBER 3, 1993, AS WINNER OF THE WILLIAM CHADWELL MEMORIAL TROPHY IN 1992, JACKIE PREPARES TO PRESENT TROPHY AND RIBBONS TO THE 1993 WINNER AT THE ESSEX FOX HOUNDS HUNTER TRIALS IN PEAPACK, NEW JERSEY.

to beat this,' I told her," recalled Jeanne Hamilton Troast. "I told her I would get Midnight ready for her. She wrote back, 'I would love for you to ride him.' "

Jeanne took Midnight with her when she moved to her new Oakleigh Farm in Green Springs, Virginia. He was injured while out in the field one day, and it took six months for him to recover. "You could play cards on his back," she said of his smooth gait. "He floated. But when he reached fifth gear and the endorphins hit, away he went. When I offered to ride him, I didn't know if I could handle him. She was a much better rider than I am."

Jeanne prepared to get up on Midnight. "I'm praying to Jackie, 'Help me with this horse.' Moments after that, Midnight was covered with yellow butterflies that came out of nowhere. I think I just got help," Jeanne says, adding, "They [the butter-flies] are the Greek symbol for the soul."

The elegant equestrian Jackie Kennedy Onassis passed away on May 19, 1994. As of this writing, at age twenty-four,

MIDNIGHT IS JACKIE'S ONLY LIVING HORSE.

OPPOSITE MIDNIGHT.

FOLLOWING SPREAD NOVEMBER 5, 1989: JACKIE WITH HER MOUNT BE FRANK.

Photograph Credits

About the Author

VICKY MOON has chronicled the lives of the rich, the not-so-rich, the famous, and the not-so-famous for more than twenty years. She has covered local murders and prominent lives in her hometown of Middleburg, Virginia, for *People Magazine* and the *Washington Post*; and written about Middleburg's hunt balls, steeplechase races, and parties for *Town and Country, Millionaire, Veranda,* and *Southern Accents* magazines. She has served as a contributing editor for *House and Garden.* Ms. Moon is the author of *The Official Middleburg Life Cookbook, The Middleburg Mystique: A Peek Inside the Gates of Middleburg, Virginia, Best Dressed Southern Salads* and *A Sunday Horse: Inside The Grand Prix Show Jumping Tour.* She lives in Middleburg, Virginia, with her husband, sportswriter Leonard Shapiro, and her son. She can be reached at www.VickyMoon.com.